Proverbs of Influence

Randy Johnson

Acknowledgment

Just this morning, I walked into a new, two-level Starbucks in Arizona. The place was beautiful, state-of-the-art, open, new, and modern. Fresh and clean with natural light showering the entire store. Amidst all that visually appealing aesthetic stood Laura, not a barista, but a Customer Support Specialist. Laura greeted me as soon as I stepped through the door. As I approached the counter, she relayed instructions and invitations to me for seating, Wi-Fi, process, how my drink was to be delivered, and overall how she was there to make my experience the best it could be! Laura was memorable! Which made my experience memorable. Which then made Starbucks in Gilbert, AZ memorable. Which is now why I'm telling my readers, and frankly anyone else who will listen…about my amazing experience. What was it about Laura that made her memorable? Laura represents really the encapsulation of the book you are about to read. She has a set of attributes that are noticeable, different, valued added, and engaging. Her behavior made me feel a certain way about the experience. How you make someone feel directly impacts trust, engagement, and influence. In 30 seconds, she created a "brand" with me that I will never forget. It sounds weird, but I will never forget her! This is why in my book you will hear detailed stories of events that happened recently, and some that happened 35 years ago. Because good experiences, people who are memorable, never are forgotten. On the flip side, the same principle is true. So, as you read this book, be open to the attributes that are just true of people who create memories. People who build trust…and people who have great influence.

I want readers to have a better understanding of their personal brand, how they are perceived, and how their brand is helping them or hurting them. Projecting them forward to higher levels of influence in their lives, or holding them back from getting all they want out of life. I hope you gain practical advice on personal attributes that when employed will set you apart in the marketplace, your school, your community, etc. I hope you will enjoy the real-life stories, and reflect on times when you have seen these attributes work in your life . I hope you gain inspiration for the real change you can make to position yourself for the highest level of influence.

I called this book the Proverbs of Influence because, throughout history, truths, and advice have been passed on to future generations through stories based on experiences and wisdom. One of the most famous sets of advice came from King Solomon, who passed on a set of principles, advice, and life wisdom through Proverbs:

Proverbs are:

Short traditional saying that shares a common TRUTH or some sort of advice.

Passed down through the generations, widely recognized as true, universal, and relatable. Similar to written proverbs, there are certain things we just know to be true in our lives. Even though we may not always agree, they still are true. Here are some examples:

Save money for a rainyday

Don't put all your eggs in one basket

You can't judge a book by its cover

Actions speak louder than words

Rome wasn't built in a day

Going into this book, I truly believe that people who adopt these principles I have seen to be true through my life, will increase their trust, their performance, their status, and ultimately their ability to influence.

Having been in a corporate environment for 40 years, 25 of them in an executive position, I have learned a lot about human behavior, influence, culture, human performance, etc. I have developed a set of beliefs that really stand the test of time, are always true, and are always effective. The ideas in the book represent the common attributes of the people I have seen develop the highest level of influence.

Why now? I feel like our world has lost many of the basic principles of human interaction, healthy disagreements, great customer service, and sometimes even general decency toward each other. We employ violence, raised voices, protests, arguing, insulting, division, clubs, gangs, squads, packs, etc. to try to convince "the other side" of our position. And it is not working. I feel this book is important to show some basic attributes that stand the test of time. That when used, will elevate a person's ability to lead, govern, convince, and bond with others. In today's world, I think the spoils go to people who can figure this out, who can do something different than the world is expecting. For instance, the world of customer service has gotten so bad, in my opinion, that when someone, anyone does something remotely positive and makes you feel like you have had a special experience, it is like a breath of fresh air. I have told my 3 boys "It doesn't take that much these days to set yourself apart." If you do, the world is your oyster. I have been encouraged to write this book by a long list of mentees who have (years later) come back to me and said "Randy, what you said to me about this or that worked for me. I am now passing that on to my co-workers, etc. You should write a book!"

So, here it is! I hope you enjoy The Proverbs of Influence!

Table of Contents

Introduction

Life has rules – okay, maybe not the best way to start this – but hey, it's the truth. Maybe we all have been told this so often that we choose to rebel at whatever chance we get. Maybe we all need to have a conversation – a one-on-one, casual, and light-hearted conversation about this. So, here I am, Randy Johnson, conversing with every reader, and penning down the bitter, hard truths about life.

Let's begin anew. See, there are some truths that exist whether we acknowledge them or not. They exist because that's how the world has been spinning around, working and basically, never needing our approval. You wouldn't step off the rooftop and expect to float, right? That's gravity in play – without asking for our approval – it just doesn't care if we believe it or not. Influence works in the same way. Influence is tied to how people perceive us, how much they trust us, and ultimately, how much they are willing to change based on what we "bring to the table". '

I'll be honest, many people still believe that their actions, personality, and the way they present themselves aren't directly related to their success. They think they should still get the promotion, close the sale, or gain respect simply because they want it, or maybe feel they deserve it. But, quite unfortunately, life works differently – quite differently from what they believe. There are unwritten rules about how people interact, how to build trust, and how to gain influence. These rules are the natural laws of influence. We have said a lot of influence, let's just first be clear about what influence is. The word has diverse meanings and interpretations today. Let's sum it up and break it down.

What is Influence?

"Influence is your capacity to get people to care about what you have to say, trust your opinions – and ultimately change their behavior that hopefully benefits them and you. Influence today is a measure of how much you matter to people – whether in the real world or on social media."

Basically, influence in a major determinant on whether you will get what you want in life. From trying to close a big sale, get your well-deserved promotion, get people to accept your ideas, or even serenade someone to go on a date with you, it is centered around the influence you wield. And at the heart of influence lies trust. Trust is the driving force of all the relationships we build and the lack of it severs our ties.

Simply put, when people trust you, they develop a likeness and tend to listen to you. They respect your opinions, look up to you, and are more likely to follow you. As we all know, trust isn't served, it has to be earned.

The trust you gain, the relationships you secure, and the consistency in carrying it all ultimately define what I like to call your 'personal brand'. You have got a brand – sounds surprising, right? Or maybe not? Yes, you have a brand or a reputation, and that brand is either helping you or hurting you.

Your Brand: Like It or Not, You Have One

Whether you realize it or not, you have a brand. It is how people perceive you, and is well-rooted in the experiences they had with you over time. Begin by acknowledging that you have a brand, and it is solely your responsibility to manage it. Letting it be haywire, not keeping tabs on it, and simply not giving the slightest thought where it's headed – will simply harm you in the long run. Here is a principle worth remembering--**If you don't manage your brand, it will manage you.**

People are in a constant tussle to achieve what they want, they spend their entire lives routing, and re-routing their paths to success – their definition of success. They work their butts off for that one promotion, but every year, they are passed over it. They will offer their best ideas, but almost every idea is dimmed by someone's not-so-bright idea. They attend every single official dinner, but they only remain surrounded by their two introverted colleagues. If you find yourself in one of those situations, here is some news, your brand is working against you!! Maybe you didn't get that promotion because the managers didn't have enough trust in you, or that bright idea didn't convey that influence. Or you couldn't connect with others because, again, people couldn't trust you enough?

But here is some good news for you. Your brand isn't set in stone. You can change it. In this book, I will give you several ideas on how to change your brand.

The Wrong Way to Influence Others

Look around at the world today, and we see a broken and deluded model of influence. Shouting is how we talk, taking an extreme stance is our first resort, and disagreement is a personal attack – we behave like predators. Steadily and strategically, we have been trained to win and overpower others. And it all has been presented as the best way forward – winning at all costs and winning any way we see fit. But here is the pertinent question, has it worked? Has it eased our lives? Has it improved our influence?

Not at all.

Divide and conquer was the way of tyrants and dictators – and shouldn't be replicated or followed. It never leads to progress. It creates more tension, more misunderstandings, and more resistance to change. History proves that true influence doesn't mean dominating a conversation, proving someone else wrong, or shouting your views – it's about listening, caring, serving, and being open to different perspectives. Influence is about building bridges, not burning them. Its about building a life that is truly influential! Not trying the same old things and wondering why you can't get what you want!

A New Model for Influence

This book presents better ways to influence, a new model of influence – a model that will surely work.

I've identified 12 proverbs—universal truths—that govern influence. Think of them as principles that have been tried and tested. Some might sting, some might seem bitter, and you might wish they weren't true, but like gravity, they exist and will continue to exist whether you believe in them or not. And if you strive to implement them into your life, you will see your life take a pleasant turn.

I know a guy, Mike. He was the guy who always said "no." No matter the idea, suggestion, or initiative, his first instinct was to resist. He was slow to adapt, seldom appreciated new ideas, and always pushed back against change. His colleagues saw him as an obstacle rather than a leader—someone who shut down discussions rather than moved them forward. Over time, people stopped seeking his input, not because he lacked intelligence or experience, but because they knew exactly what his response would be. His reputation…his brand… became that of a roadblock, not a team player, and it started to cost him opportunities.

One day, after our coaching session, Mike decided to ask his coworkers an honest question: "What do you think my reputation is?" The answers weren't flattering. But instead of getting defensive, he listened. He realized that his brand was holding him back. So, he finally decided to make a change.

By incorporating several of the proverbs in this book, he shifted his approach. He became more open, more adaptable, and more supportive of his team's ideas. In short, he became influential! Within a year, people started noticing the change. That change didn't just get him noticed, it improved his relationships at work and ultimately got him the promotion he had been chasing for years. At the writing of this book, Mike is a Director for a large company and enjoying great success.

What This Book Will Do for You

Look, this might come off as asking you to 'change yourself' but this isn't about changing who you are — it is all about helping you become the best version of yourself. It's about recognizing the laws of influence – the universal truths – and implementing them to build trust, strengthen relationships, and achieve what you want in life.

Each of the 12 proverbs enlisted in this book is based on simple, practical wisdom that you can apply in your life. Some of this wisdom may challenge your current mindset. Others may help you affirm what you have always known. But all of them will help you become more influential – or as is popularly said, be the best version of yourself.

So, are you ready to take control of your brand? Are you ready to build more trust? Get ready to create stronger connections and achieve your goals with greater ease.

Let's get started.

Chapter 1
Personal Brand – Current State of my Reputation

Let's break down personal brand. In simpler words –

"Your personal brand is like your reputation, it's how you show up online and in real life. It's the vibe people get from you based on what you say, do, and share."

"The cool thing about a personal brand is you can shape it however you want. But right now, you might be unknowingly letting things like your online profile or how you act around people create that brand for you."

But What Exactly is a Personal Brand?

By a typical definition, *'personal brand is the belief people hold about you based on the experiences they have with you over time.'* Whether you are trying to sell something, pitch your ideas, secure a promotion, or simply trying to gain trust, your personal brand influences all of it.

Think about it—if you're consistently late on assignments, delaying commitments, or postponing your plans, people will start to believe that you're unreliable. People who have such unpleasant interactions will converse about you in the same manner. Eventually, that belief grows, mushrooming your ill-repute, and ultimately defining your brand. And once your brand is set, it either helps you significantly or hinders you catastrophically.

Being known as unreliable will surely work against you especially when you are looking for trust or support. The reality is that all your actions, reactions, gestures, notions, nudges, and conversations over time are the building blocks for your personal brand.

Think of it as building a fort. One person might create a fort with strong, secure walls — walls made of trust, consistency, and kindness. These walls protect the fort from any outside negativity and make it a safe place for others to trust and rely on. On the contrary, someone might build a fort with walls that seem strong but are actually harmful. Maybe they're built with arrogance, dishonesty, or a lack of consideration for others. Over time, those walls end up hurting the person inside the fort, creating a reputation that makes it hard for people to trust or connect with them.

So, when you're building your personal brand, think about the walls you're putting up. Are they protecting you and building trust, or are they hurting your reputation and isolating you?

Pro-tip: Follow through your commitments and regularly review your brand.

Common Misconceptions About Personal Branding

"It doesn't matter" – oof, the causal carelessness. Be careful with this belief.

"It doesn't matter how people see me" – well, yeah, when it comes to self-confidence, sure.

"It doesn't matter if they trust me or not" – oh, but, it does. It does a lot.

"It doesn't matter if their vibe doesn't match" – sure if we're talking about jamming together. But otherwise . . .

Think about it: online influencers build their entire presence around a brand, carefully curating their image to gain more followers. But in the grand scheme of things, is your online brand where you want it to be? Are you building influence in a way that truly benefits you, or just chasing likes and validation? Your digital presence is an extension of your real-world reputation, and whether you realize it or not, it's influencing how people see and interact with you.

Many believe that their choices — be it punctuality, work ethic, communication style, or interactions with others — don't affect their ability to influence. Over the years, I've worked with many individuals who didn't have the slightest idea why they weren't getting what they wanted out of life – why their lives were crumbling, why they kept "hitting walls". When I introduced the concept of personal branding, it was like seeing the fresh and first light of the day. For the longest time, they thought their personal brand wasn't theirs, but when they saw tangible ways to improve it, they embraced it wholly.

I repeat why I am writing this book – to make you aware of your own brand. Just throw this notion of 'I don't have a brand' in the trash bin because trust me, you do. And let's move on to the important questions.

Do you know what your brand is? Can you define it for me or yourself? More importantly, if you know what it is, are you happy with it? If not, it's time to make some changes at the grassroots. In the following chapters, I will introduce 12 proverbs that, when applied, will strengthen your brand and enhance your ability to influence others.

Pro Tip: Your personal brand isn't what you say it is – it's what others perceive it to be. Every action, every interaction, and even your silence shapes it. Own your narrative.

The Role of Branding in Decision-Making

As a senior leader, I am often asked to make high-stakes decisions with limited information.

This act of difficult decisions is often practiced when it comes to promotions, leadership opportunities, or project approvals. After spending 25 years in executive boardrooms, I can assure you I've witnessed hundreds of these discussions firsthand and have sometimes dreaded these decisions. It's like you must make someone's day and break someone's heart because there are always half a dozen people expecting to the same role. But there can only be one. We executives make our nemesis that way.

Imagine a leadership team gathered to discuss a potential promotion:

"I'd like to promote Sally to Director. Any objections?"

In most cases, the executives don't pull out detailed reports or performance reviews. Instead, they reflect on their past interactions with Sally. Well, interactions are the firsthand reports we executives have.

The responses are usually "Yeah, I can see that. She's a great performer and a great culture fit."

And just like that—Sally gets the promotion.

If you think its more complicated than that, its really not. Why? Because of her brand. Her reputation is remarkable, was built over time, and influenced the decision-makers when it mattered most.

People often ask me, "What does it take to get promoted?" The answer is simple: manage your brand. Every interaction you have with an executive, a colleague, or a client shapes their perception of you. And those seemingly trivial interactions are what matters the most. When that life-changing moment arrives, your brand will be the determining factor.

Pro Tip: Decisions about your future are often made when you're not in the room. Build a brand so strong that when your name comes up, the answer is an easy "yes."

Take Control of Your Brand

Here is honest advice. In life, we want to control everything, we all like a certain control over things, even those that are way out of our range of control. Given the chance, we would even want to control how our day or even week ahead should look. But here is the honest truth, we don't have control over everything, even the things that we own. We don't control the people we love, we control behaviors, we don't control our day, and sometimes we don't have control over ourselves.

We have to let go of things to have a little peace in our lives. Nitpicking everything, tinkering with every frivolous matter, and making a huge deal out of tiny details, will most certainly drive us crazy. Choose to ignore things in life that don't matter too much.

Your personal brand is what matters so much. It is not something you can afford to ignore. It affects your opportunities, relationships, and overall success. The good news is that you have the power to shape it, and in return, your personal brand defines your success.

In the chapters ahead, I will introduce 12 proverbs—time-tested principles that will help you refine and strengthen your personal brand. By incorporating these truths into your daily life, you will build trust, increase your influence, and unlock new opportunities.

Your brand is your most valuable asset. Your brand is your identity. Your brand is what makes or breaks your personal and professional lives. Let's make sure it is working for you, not against you.

Pro Tip: You can't control everything in life, but you can control how you show up. Own your brand with intention — because if you don't shape it, someone else will.

Practical Takeaways

✓ Every action, no matter how small, contributes to your personal brand.

- ✓ Identify your current brand — ask yourself: What do people believe about me? Are these perceptions helping or hindering me?

- ✓ Remember, branding is not about perfection; it's about consistency and authenticity.

Exercises

- ➢ Sentence Exercise: Write a single sentence describing how you believe others perceive you today. Compare it to how you want to be perceived and identify gaps.

  For example: How I believe others perceive me today: "John is reliable and hardworking, but he tends to avoid leadership roles and stays in the background."

  How I want to be perceived: "John is a confident leader who takes initiative and inspires others with his vision."

  Gap identified: I need to step out of my comfort zone, voice my ideas more often, and take on leadership opportunities to shift my brand from being just reliable to being seen as a leader.

- ➢ Journaling Prompt: Reflect on recent interactions — what did your actions communicate about your brand?

- ➢ Self-Assessment Checklist: Evaluate your brand in areas such as timeliness, communication, professionalism, and relationships.

➢ Discover Your Brand: Your personal brand already exists — whether you've intentionally shaped it or not. It's the perception others have of you, based on your actions, words, and presence. Let's take a moment to evaluate where you stand.

Step 1: Gather Honest Feedback

Identify **five** of your closest colleagues, friends, or members of your inner circle. Ask each of them to describe you **honestly** in **one sentence.** Encourage them to be truthful, not just polite.

Step 2: Reflect on Their Responses

Once you have all five sentences, take a step back and analyze them:

- Are you **comfortable** with how others see you?

- Does this **align** with how you want to be perceived?

- Is this **helping or hurting** your influence, opportunities, and relationships?

Step 3: Shape Your Brand with the Right Proverbs

As you read this book, think about the **12 proverbs** and how they apply to your personal brand.

- Which ones **already** reflect who you are?

- Which ones do you **want to incorporate** to strengthen your influence?

- What small shifts can you make today to **reshape your brand** in a positive direction?

Chapter 2
Proverb #1 – Show up consistently memorable

Vision board-ers, assemble! Do you own an online or a physical vision board hanging at the top of your desk, haunting you every single day? Well, did your last year's vision board look something similar to the one above? How many 'goals' did you actually achieve and tick off from that vision board?

I apologize if this comes off as 'contemptuous', it is anything but 'making fun of your vision board' or 'taunting' you for having one. Like I said, this is going to be a conversation, and will always be a casual conversation. Take this as a banter, one of my 'late night banters' on vision board-ers.

But here is what you need to hear the most,

"Sit back, relax. You're too stressy."

"Don't be a buzzkill. Go with the flow. Let it go."

Unbelievable, I would be quoting teenagers to convince you to, yes, do let it go sometimes. Life, more like time, will never ever, ever be in our control. The moment you define this is what you want to achieve in such and such timeline, life will bombard you with surprises – unpleasant, uncomfortable, and quite frustrating surprises. In no way, life is becoming predictable, and not even in a thousand years, you are gaining complete control over your life.

Take that in. Take a moment and accept that truth wholeheartedly.

Pro-Tip: Embrace the unpredictability of life!

The Myth of Traditional Goal-Setting

"Set goals. You are nothing without knowing your goals."

"You need to have goals to have a purposeful life."

"Goals are the stepping stones to success. No goals, no success."

I feel 'stressy' writing these down. I truly understand how one must feel who is consistently and relentlessly told to achieve your goals, or have goals, or called a failure for not achieving goals. You are, and will always be, more than your 'goals'. Your goals will never define your worth.

With that being said, let's logically, rationally, and with evidence dump this goal-setting myth. Firstly, we, as humans, have an urge to hype up everything we freshly learn. When we must have learned about 'goals', we took it and overdramatized it. Pick up any book, pick up any podcast or Tedtalk related to 'how to get successful', they won't get tired of telling you how goal-setting is synonymous to breathing. Yes – sadly – goal-setting is widely accepted as the foundation of success. We're persistently told to write down our dreams, set SMART goals, and map out our futures. But here's the reality — brace yourselves – goals without action lead to frustration, disappointment, and a decline in self-esteem. Here is another truth, having goals is not the issue; the problem arises when we focus too much on the *outcome* rather than the *process* that gets us there. And everyone and every book that talks about 'goals' talks only about the

OUTCOME as if the process is not worthwhile to go through. Consider this. Let's test that theory when it comes to influence-- Ask yourself and ask people around you, how they got to their current level of influence. Did they, at an early age, ever dream of being where they are, doing what they are doing, etc.? The answer generally is NO. I could not have fathomed a goal that would have had me where I am today. Now, there are a rare few who say they want to be a doctor, or an astronaut, etc and then become one. But at your next social gathering, test my theory and ask the question. I think you will find that most of us just dive in, embrace what life has for us, and we progress. And we end up where we are today. Im asking you to consider that goals don't get you there, putting in the work, and showing up memorable every day does.

Joshua Medcalf and Jamie Gilbert's book, *Burn Your Goals*, introduced a countercultural approach to success—one that resonated deeply with my own life experience. Their philosophy? It's not about setting goals; it's about the way you show up every single day. Excellence isn't achieved through an end goal but through consistent effort, discipline, and commitment to mastering the fundamentals.

Tell me if that doesn't make our lives easier. Tell me that isn't really how most people get to the level of influence that currently enjoy. It's unfortunate how easily and casually we disregard the act of 'showing up every day.' But we all want the best version, the utmost effort, the highest numbers, and the most conversions every single day from every single person.

Pro-Tip: Instead of fixating solely on end goals, focus on cultivating daily habits and processes that align with your values.

My Journey: From Small-Town Student to Senior Executive

I know, what you must be thinking now. Here comes the 'pity story' of this guy. Or there is always a 'humble' beginning for every person who wrote a book. And yes, there is always a story. Everyone has one – you too have a story, no matter how humble or not. Never disregard your journey, never undersell your story, and never toss the tale of struggles away. After all, it is all we have and what makes us, us.

So, here is my story.

I grew up in a small farming community in Minnesota, an average student in a class of 29. I wasn't an exceptional athlete or a standout scholar. Just an average kid. If you had asked anyone back then, they wouldn't have predicted I'd achieve anything remarkable. And yet, I spent 25 of my 40-year career in executive leadership roles. But how did that happen? I am not and never have been a detailed 'goal-setting' mapper. But I learned the three simple principles to live by. Here are my magical, grand, tried-and-tested, and surefire ways to achieve success:

1.   **Outwork everyone around me.**

2.   **Always do more than what's expected. Make someone say "wow" for the right reasons!**

3.   **Add value by producing meaningful results daily.**

But work ethic isn't everything, you need to have an added skill to sail your boat smoothly. I developed a strong emotional intelligence — Most people would describe me as adept at reading situations, understand unspoken emotions, and building relationships that mattered. These qualities led me from Sales to Human Resources, to Administration, and ultimately, to Executive Leadership.

My influence, my achievements were not the outcome of a meticulously crafted career plan. Or a vision board guiding me in my professional life. It was the result of showing up, putting in the work, and doing the little things that impacted others significantly — day in and day out.

Pro- tip: Goals are important. But decide now how you will show up every day. Embrace the daily grind. Trust the process. You will get to a higher level of influence than your goal statement could have ever dreamt possible. Promise.

Shift Your Focus: Process Over Outcome

Look, you cannot summit Mt. Everest just by staring at its picture or watching documentaries about it. You cannot become the best athlete out there just by 'wanting' to become one. You need to take those small steps that take you closer every day to your bigger goal, or milestone – whatever you call it.

Kobe Bryant, a household name and a name synonymous with success, will be the perfect example of this type of mindset. He dreamt of becoming the greatest, he dreamt the dream every single day. But he knew 'just dreaming' to be the greatest wouldn't get him anywhere — he knew he had to put in relentless effort every single day to make it happen. And he did exactly that.

From a young age, Kobe was obsessed with improving his game. He followed the "Mamba Mentality" — a commitment to continuous growth, discipline, and hard work. While other players might have solely relied on their talent, Kobe outworked them all. He practiced before dawn, studied film, and constantly refined his skills. He once famously said, "Great things come from hard work and perseverance. No excuses."

This aligns perfectly with the idea that you can't reach the summit of your goals just by looking at your fancy vision board. You have to take deliberate steps every day, you might have to sacrifice more than you assumed just to move closer to your goal. Kobe didn't just wish to be great; he *worked* to be great, and that's what set him apart. 2020 was a tough year for all of us, and losing Kobe was another blow we all weren't ready for. He left us physically, but his mentality, hard work, and dedication will live eternally as an example for us.

So, the point is, if you want to maximize your potential, shift your focus away from rigid goal-setting and toward purposeful daily actions. Fixating too much on a specific outcome will stress you out, and divert you from mastering the habits and disciplines that will naturally lead you to success.

Take a look at your own life. Did you end up exactly where you envisioned yourself? Most people don't. They end up where their consistent efforts, decisions, and adaptability take them. It's not the 'goal on the vision board' that determines success; it's the daily grind you put in along the way.

Pro-tip: Success isn't about grand moments; it is about the small, daily, non-negotiable actions – it is about consistent efforts.

Addressing the Risks: Vision Without Rigidity

To be clear, I'm not suggesting you be rudderless. I am not saying not to be passionate about something or go on without a sense of direction. Vision, passion, and direction are essential, for sure. But the key is to not become so fixated on a specific goal that you miss greater opportunities along the way. Be adaptable.

Adaptability means accepting change, learning from setbacks, and adjusting your approach as you go along the way. Life is unpredictable, and being rigid about your life's trajectory can significantly limit your growth. The most successful people aren't just those who set goals — they are those who recognize when to pivot, seize unexpected opportunities, and evolve with new circumstances.

Think of it like summiting Mount Everest. Do you think it's a smooth climb, or you might know the exact path to its peak? No, you may start with a clear path in mind, but as you climb, you might encounter obstacles — fallen trees, cliffs, unexpected weather, or tiredness, above all. A rigid climber might insist on sticking to their original route, even if it delays their summit or no longer is the best option. An adaptable climber, however, will reassess, find a new path, and keep moving forward without losing sight of the ultimate destination.

The same principle applies to life. Your vision and passion give you direction, but your ability to adapt, learn, and grow tells how far you will actually go.

So, instead, adopt a mindset of adaptability:

- **Set a vision, but don't let it confine you.**
- **Work hard and go above and beyond in everything you do.**
- **Be open to unexpected opportunities that come from your efforts.**

If I had rigidly stuck to a single career goal, I would have never experienced the diverse opportunities that shaped my life. I went from Agriculture to Accounting, to Health Care, to Non-Profit, to Retail Equipment, to Construction, and then to Energy. Never in my wildest dreams, did they include that career path and trajectory. And no bigger goal could have predicted that path. But my core philosophy—working hard, adding value, and staying open to opportunity—ensured I thrived in every industry I entered. I got to experience things I could have never experienced if I had stuck to one industry – and I am grateful for the path my efforts took me.

Pro-tip: Adaptability isn't losing direction; it's finding a better route when the road ahead changes.

Do the Work, and Success Will Follow

Big goal, bigger dream, bigger house, bigger car, bigger this and bigger that - it's easy to fall into the trap of obsessing over 'big' goals. Have big goals, sure, but don't ever disregard and underestimate the small steps and daily success you achieve. Think of it this way: If you want to build muscle, you don't just set a goal to be fit and hope for the jacked-up body. You show up at the gym, lift weights, eat right, and stay disciplined day after day – consistently and relentlessly. The same goes for financial success, you don't just dream of wealth—you've to master your craft, make smart financial decisions, add value wherever you go, build better professional relationships, and then get to that bigger goal. It's always the small steps that count.

Be it career, influence, or financial, growth will never be one big break. It's about the daily stumbles, unglamorous habits, getting back up, defeating procrastination, telling yourself to do what you got to do, and never giving up every day that build momentum over time. Consider whether your current brand is described as outworking others, adding value, and doing more than expected every day. If not, are you willing to give it a try and starting giving people around you a different experience…changing your brand…and increasing your influence?

Remember:

- **Master the fundamentals.** Whatever field you're in, get exceptionally good at the basics. The best athletes, musicians, and leaders spend years refining their foundational skills.

- **Add value to everything you do.** Approach everything in your life with a 'contribution mindset.' Whether it is your job, relationships, or personal growth, think about how you can contribute more and make it better. The more you give, the more opportunities come your way.

- **Be relentless.** Success doesn't come from occasional bursts of motivation—and no one is motivated every day year-round. So, show up and put in the work every single day, even when you don't feel like it.

Pro-tip: Stop fixating on the end result and start mastering the process. The rest will take care of itself.

Practical Takeaways

- ✓ Success stems from consistent daily effort, not just goal-setting.

- ✓ Embrace the grind — focus on adding value, working hard, and exceeding expectations.

- ✓ Goals should guide, not limit. Stay flexible and seize opportunities that arise from your work.

- ✓ The journey matters more than the destination; results follow purposeful actions.

Exercises

- ➤ Reflection Exercise: Think back to high school. Did you imagine yourself in your current role? Likely not. Reflect on how your daily efforts, not rigid goals, shaped your path. How can you repeat those things that have worked for you?

➢ Daily Action Plan: Write down three small, purposeful actions you can take today to add value and exceed expectations in your work or life.

➢ Vision Check: Identify a broad vision for your life or career. List ways to enjoy the process of working toward it without being tied to specific outcomes.

Chapter 3
Proverb #2 – Choose an 'I Am Second' Mentality once in a while

Before you misinterpret, 'I am second' doesn't imply putting yourself last and letting others run you over or letting others take the opportunities that you deserve. Some might take this as putting others as a priority and ignoring your goals, needs, ambitions, and vision. Well, to be honest, if taken literally, 'I am second' could mean zero self-care, constantly sacrificing your growth, backburning your vision, and devoting yourself to serving others – literally.

However, this is not the true meaning of the "I am second" mindset. It is not about diminishing yourself, disregarding your needs, and letting others take away your well-deserved opportunities. If we put it in a definition, 'I am second' means, 'choosing to serve others selflessly and prioritize their success in a way that ultimately benefits you both.'

Here is another way to look at it. The 'I am second' mentality is about building influence by finding fulfillment in helping others reach their potential. It is about putting others' needs ahead of your own in key moments—not in a way that hurts your trajectory to success, but in a way that supports mutual growth and success.

The key, as always, is balance. A balance between how you must still care for yourself, set boundaries, and pursue your own goals while helping others achieve the same. The 'I am second' mentality means being willing to step back occasionally, choose to support others, and shift your focus to their needs when the situation calls for it – all this without losing sight of your purpose and without sacrificing your well-being.

Pro-tip: 'I am second' mentality means strategic service, not self-sacrifice. Support others, keep your vision in sight, and create mutual opportunities.

The 'I Am Second' Mentality

Adopting an *'I am second'* mindset means shifting your focus from personal gain to helping others excel. Many of the most influential leaders, coaches, and mentors adopt this approach, knowing that only by elevating others, they can build stronger relationships, trust, and long-term success. Whether it's professional life or personal, we, as human beings, need each other to succeed. Take any biggest corporations in the world, say Amazon, was it built only by one person? Yes, the idea might have been exclusive to one person, but without the help of hundreds of people, their commitment, and trust in each other, Amazon wouldn't be standing where it stands now. And let me tell you, some people had this 'I am second' mindset that made Amazon an amazing multi-billion-dollar company.

Anyone who knows me knows that I am a huge golf fan. I played it in college, play it every chance I get. I was lucky enough to have three boys who loved the sport, excelled at it, and played it at a very high level. Even though I have my favorites, I have always been amazed at the caddies and the mentality they bring to the game. They exist to serve the player. To ensure that all aspects of a player's decisions, equipment, resources needed, etc. are ready for them to perform at their highest possible level. They carry a heavy bag for hours on end. They know more about the course than even the player. They are the picture of the consummate servant, "I am second" mentality. They get their greatest joy knowing that their efforts led to a player's success. What is that mentality? It is the mentality that I don't always have to be the "player" but I can find great joy and purpose in serving. It's a mentality that I gain power and respect by giving it away to others. At the end of the 2024 Masters, when Scottie Scheffler had performed at a level worthy of eclipsing the field, and he had won the Masters for a second time, he was walking off the 18th green and stopped – allowing his caddy Ted Scott time to catch up to him and walk shoulder to shoulder to the Butler cabin, where Scottie was to don his second "green jacket". The pinnacle of any golfer's dream career. The lessons in this example are probably endless, one of which for our current or future self as a leader. So, why is a caddy or I am second mentality worth a spot in my 12 proverbs? Because it's about influence. Arguably, the caddie has as much influence to a player's success as the player making the swings. And Scottie Scheffler knew this and waited for Ted to join him on the walk to the Butler cabin. In our lives, we will not always be the "player". Taking an I am second, or a caddy mentality can and will position us as a servant, providing us joy, pride, achievement and ultimately influence if we look at it correctly. Great caddies do and so should we.

To simplify this: Think about the last time someone truly helped you—not for their gain, but simply to see you succeed. Maybe it was a mentor who guided you in your career, a teacher who went the extra mile to help you understand a subject or even a friend who supported you during a tough time. We all have encountered one or more people who have done good to us, without seeking their own gain. Their influence likely left a lasting impact, not because they demanded recognition, but because they genuinely prioritized your success. I recall that person as I write, I know I will remember that person's face for the rest of my life. And I know you remember your person too.

Did that person help you to achieve their gain? Did that person help you as a return favor? Or did that person help you expecting something in return? The reason their help had such a profound effect on us is that they genuinely only helped us – no gain, no return favor, no expectations – they truly just helped us. This is the 'I am second' mentality we all need.

Pro-tip: Selflessly help others succeed, which in turn will build trust, influence, and most importantly, meaningful relationships.

The Caddy's Role: A Lesson in Selfless Service

Let's go back to the caddy example.

A caddy's job isn't to be the star of the show — it's to support the golfer by offering guidance, encouragement, and practical assistance. Yes, the golfer puts in the effort, practices every day, and tries his best to win an event, but without a caddy supporting him or her, even the best golfer might stumble.

The caddy's role is a lesson in selfless service. The caddy doesn't even get pictured when the golfer receives the trophy, but he does it all for that one key moment that matters the most – winning together. This is the essence of servant leadership: prioritizing others' success, to achieve greater influence and fulfillment. Just like a caddy, true leaders understand that serving others doesn't make you weaker — it makes you indispensable.

Pro-tip: The more you serve selflessly and elevate those around you, the greater your influence and fulfillment will be in the long run.

The Power of Servant Leadership

We are, naturally and traditionally, trained to consider our reporting authorities as our 'boss'. Boss, the one with power, authority, and all the right to fire you whenever he desires. We all have met 'bosses' in our lives, and we all equally despise their existence.

Imagine this 'boss' turns over a new leaf. I mean, instead of hammering you down with deadlines, threats of demotions, and forcing you to work after shift, this 'boss' hands you your well-deserved promotion – and that too, without you begging for it. Or this 'boss' guides you on how you can get to that promotion. Unreal, right? That is just the tip of how servant leadership can be.

Servant leadership primarily focuses on the growth and well-being of others. Unlike traditional leadership where the leader is all-powerful, servant leadership flips the script. It places the leader's role as a servant first – not literal servant – supporting and empowering others to achieve their fullest potential. A servant leader will ensure that the people they lead are equipped, motivated, and empowered to succeed. It fosters an environment of trust, collaboration, and respect, where people feel valued and heard. This kind of leadership creates a culture where everyone, from the leader to the team, works together toward mutual success. This is the kind of leadership that keeps people happy to work and feel motivated to be at their workplace.

As you consider the Proverbs in this book, what about the "I am Second" principle? Are you willing to make this a part of your brand? Do you want to be known for, at key times, being the caddy and not the player? Give it a try…your influence will grow as a result!

Pro-tip: Shift your mindset from "I'm the boss" to
"How can I help my team succeed?"

Key Principles of Servant Leadership

1. **Empathy**
   Servant leaders understand and share the feelings of others. They take the time to listen and understand the needs, concerns, and challenges of those they lead. This empathy builds trust and deepens relationships.

2. **Listening**
   Servant leaders don't just hear words — they listen actively and with the intent to understand. This creates an open, transparent environment where others feel comfortable sharing their thoughts and ideas.

3. **Stewardship**
   A servant leader sees themselves as a caretaker of their team or organization. They take responsibility for the well-

being and success of those around them, ensuring that resources are used wisely and people are nurtured and developed.

4. **Commitment to the Growth of People**

    Servant leaders are dedicated to helping others grow. Whether through training, mentorship, or providing opportunities for advancement, they are committed to the personal and professional development of their team members.

Pro-tip: Effective leadership thrives on others' well-being, not on the leader's recognition.

How to Become a Servant Leader

Well, there isn't a manual on how to be the best servant leader but here are some traits that one must adopt.

1. **Lead with Humility:** Recognize that leadership is not about being in the spotlight – it's about empowering those around you. Focus on the needs of your team rather than your recognition.

2. **Serve First:** Embrace the idea that your role as a leader is to serve those you lead. Whether it's helping with a task, offering guidance, or simply being present, focus on supporting others in their growth and success.

3. **Ask the Right Questions:** Instead of dictating, ask how you can help your team. Encourage open communication and make sure everyone has a chance to be heard.

4. **Celebrate the Success of Others:** Instead of seeking personal accolades, celebrate the success of those you lead. Acknowledge their hard work and contributions to foster a sense of pride and motivation within the team.

Pro-tip: Successful leadership is determined by the team's well-being, conducive work culture, and empowered people.

Practical Takeaways

- ✓ Serve others without compromising your own progress or goals.
- ✓ Help others grow by offering support and encouragement, knowing their success strengthens your influence.
- ✓ Maintain healthy boundaries to prioritize self-care while helping others.

✓ Ensure both your success and others' success through collaborative opportunities.

✓ Find joy in others' achievements to build deeper, trust-based relationships.

✓ Stay flexible, and shift focus when needed for the greater good.

✓ Regularly assess how your support impacts others, reinforcing your role as a servant leader.

Exercises

➢ Daily Acts of Service: Identify one action each day to support or uplift someone around you.

➢ Reflection Exercise: Journal about a time you served someone and how it impacted both of you.

➢ Assess your willingness to serve by reflecting on these questions:

• Am I genuinely happy for others' successes?

• Can I find fulfillment in seasons of service?

• Do I prioritize the needs of others over my own?

Chapter 4
Proverb #3 – Learn the Art of Wow

If we just take a look around, we will find everyone just rushing—rushing to work, rushing through meetings, rushing to finish tasks, and even rushing through their personal lives. We tend to consume ourselves with "Who has got time?"

We are in a race, and "There's so much to do." There always be so much to do, and in this fast-paced world, we forget to be present in the moment, let alone go beyond what's required. Conversations are transactional, service is robotic, and gestures of kindness feel like rare relics of the past. Adding to our less-like-human interactions, there's a whole world suffering – a part of it burning, a part of it being oppressed, a part of it lost in war, and a part of it just glaring at the rest of the world with silent despair, wondering if anyone cares.

The point is, the world is getting harsher, colder, robotic, and not-human-like. And quite amusingly, humans are responsible for this. We made our world meaner for us, we made our surroundings suffocating for us, we developed this never-ending rat race of 'who's the best', 'who's the most powerful', and 'who will win this race'. There is no race. We humans are designed to live with each other, through each other's help, and pick each other up. More than that, we, as humans, have an innate urge to make others happy, a desire to see people around us filled with glee. We, as humans, cherish cheering and celebrating others. No wonder, we feel better when our kindness makes someone's day – or vice versa. But no, we choose to rush through our lives, spending every day like a robot, not pausing to look around.

But imagine if, instead of rushing through life, we took a moment to slow down and truly see the people around us. Imagine if we made an effort to notice opportunities to add a little extra care, a little extra thoughtfulness. You know, to make someone's day. It doesn't take much—an unexpected thank-you note, a small but thoughtful gesture, or simply remembering a detail about someone's life. These moments, though seemingly small, hold incredible power. They break the monotony, the cyclic predictability of routine they add a little bit of warmth in our lives – the one we often crave in our rather cold surroundings. More than that, they connect us emotionally – you do kindness, and in return, you will receive kindness – maybe manifold. Most importantly, they wow. And when we "wow" someone, our influence grows—guaranteed.

I call this the Art of Wow and it isn't about grand gestures and expensive exchanges. It is about intentionality – your intention of doing something out of routine, your intent on creating delight when people are just trying to push through their predictable lives. It is the intention that counts, remember that.

Yes, the world might not get 'happier', or in a far-fetched future, it will become better. But presently, a lot must be carried out to paint the world in bright colors or silence the chaos megaphoned around us. Still, every once in a while, something breaks through the noise—a simple, unexpected act of kindness that restores our faith in humanity.

Let me tell you a story. The year was 1991, I was traveling in Ames, IA, staying at the Gateway Holiday Inn. It was late fall, and I awoke to an unexpected snow storm. Because this was unexpected, I was obviously unprepared. I had no jacket, no gloves, and nothing to scrape ice and snow from my windshield. As I tried my best to get ready to go to my car and do my best with a rolled-up newspaper under my arm, I heard a steady purr-like sound of a cat sleeping. I opened my blinds to see an elderly man, employed by the hotel behind the "reins" of a snowblower. He was blowing a path to every car in the parking lot. Once he reached the car, he scraped the windshield of every car. What was the first word out of my mouth? WOW. That… is value, that… is being different. That is doing something the customer doesn't expect. And here I am 34 years later, remembering every detail of that morning. I remember how I felt. Where do you think I stayed every time I went to Ames? Do you think I cared about the rate they charged me?

Take, for example, Walt Disney. In the early years of building his entertainment empire, Disney insisted that every park visitor should experience something magical beyond their expectations. His attention to detail, from spotless streets to friendly cast members made each guest feel special. His philosophy of exceeding expectations turned Disneyland into the "Happiest Place on Earth." Disney understood that people don't just remember the rides—they remember how they felt. This commitment to wowing customers created lifelong fans and established an unshakable brand legacy. To this day, kids and adults alike, travel for miles and wish to be a part of the Disney experience.

Talking about traveling, think about checking into a hotel after a long journey. You know the process—a key card, a generic welcome, and directions to your room. But how do you feel if instead, the receptionist greets you warmly, leaves a handwritten note wishing you a great stay. That small effort makes that hotel, and receptionist memorable and you might have the best hotel experience only because of that small gesture.

We've all experienced such moments—times when someone, whether that's your friend, your partner, or your colleague, goes beyond the basics and leaves a lasting impression. These moments are never by a happy co-incidence; they are always an intentional effort, and a product of attention to detail, and a want to make a difference. Creating a "wow" moment means doing more than what is expected. It is that little care, a bit more attention, and a tad bit of creativity that make people remember you.   And it works everywhere, in business, leadership, and personal relationships. People who keenly practice the Art of Wow establish trust, loyalty, and, most importantly, an indelible personal brand.

Pro-tip: The Art of Wow is about adding small, meaningful touches to everyday interactions — stand out by doing the unexpected, and you'll create lasting impressions.

Small Gestures, Big Impact

I know a few of you might be coming up with the grandest gesture to please everyone. No, don't try to move mountains to wow someone. Remember, it is the intention that counts. And most likely, your grandest gesture might not wow a few people – people might raise their brows for such a gesture. Keep it simple, keep it small, keep it heartfelt, and keep it intentional. Keep the bigger-than-life gesture for yourself, or someone you like – such gestures aren't for everybody. People might start wondering how to reciprocate that gesture, like how to match that gesture, when they want to create a wow moment. Don't go overboard, don't overdo it – it is an overkill.

Here's another story. My wife and I had late morning tickets to an event in Phoenix. We figured we would have time for a late breakfast, knowing that we may not get lunch. So, we stopped at First Watch, a well-known breakfast place in Gilbert, AZ. Sitting down, I laid my keys, sunglasses, and tickets on the table. The experience was good. Good friendly server, good quality food, but let's face it, many breakfast places can do that. That is not that hard to duplicate. What happened next is very hard to duplicate.

In the middle of eating our breakfast, the server came to our table with the check, a to-go box and two travel cups for our coffee. She said "Sir, I couldn't help notice that you have tickets to an event later this morning. As I looked at the time, I wanted to make sure you got there on time, so please use these if you need them to make sure that I don't delay you. Please enjoy the event, and thanks for coming to First Watch. What was the first word I said to my wife when the server left the table? WOW. How big do you think her tip was? Do you think we are going to any other breakfast place in Gilbert, AZ? So, oftentimes, the simplest gestures have the greatest effect.

Nice story, but how do we do this in a corporate setting? Consider these examples:

• The Thoughtful Employee: You're assigned a task that involves mailing out documents. Not many of us like such a task but you decide to be creative with this task and make it a bit 'personal' for others. Instead of just printing and passing them along, you self-address an envelope for your boss to save them time. It's a small step, but it shows foresight and initiative, and garners appreciation from others.

• The Considerate Coworker: A team member is struggling to complete a project. You sit with them and talk about the problem they are facing. Believe me, even such conversations are a huge relief and the kindest you can be with your colleague. Or maybe you want to help a little more. So, you take a few extra minutes to personalize their report with a well-designed cover page or summary, making their work shine.

• The Unforgettable Customer Experience: I cannot emphasize the value of good customer experience. Trust me when I say this, there will be people who will shop at your business only because of your personal touch to their parcels or products. Even if they receive a faulty product, they will forgive and forget for the sake of 'small gestures' your business offers. Consider sending handwritten thank-you notes to customers instead of automated emails. This personal touch makes clients feel valued and increases loyalty.

Pro-tip: Every small gesture creates a ripple effect. They aren't grand gestures, but they resonate deeply because they show effort and consideration beyond what's expected.

Cultivating a Wow Mindset

What separates ordinary from extraordinary? A little bit of extra – an extra bit of detail, an extra bit of care, and a tad bit more attention. Remember, a little bit of extra, nothing too much, and absolutely nothing too majestic. It is about noticing the small, meaningful opportunities that often get overlooked and making the most of them. It is never about exhausting efforts that take up days and a little too much of your time.

Consider the story of Zappos, the online shoe retailer known for its incredible customer service. Imagine being known for customer service – such a privilege. Consider a scenario, one customer called to return a pair of shoes for her late husband. Instead of just processing the refund, the Zappos representative went a step further – a bit of care, a touch of warmth. The company not only arranged for a free return pickup but also sent flowers and a heartfelt note of condolence. How can they not have customers that stick with them for years? Trust me, I would stick with them, regardless. That unexpected act of kindness turned a routine transaction into a lifelong memory. This is the Art of Wow — small, thoughtful, and profound gestures making an indelible impact. When you start viewing the world through the lens of 'How can I contribute?', or 'How can I add something a little extra?' you shift from mere routine to spreading joy, adding value, and creating unshakable connections.

Here's how you can cultivate this mindset and make the *Art of Wow* a natural part of your life:

1. Pay Attention to Details: Noticing the small details never went out of style and will never stop being impressive. So, observe what is being overlooked, listen closely to people's wishes, and frustrations, and find ways to be there for others.

2. Think One Step Ahead: Think about how you can be a part of making someone's day or experience a memorable one – be it a small gesture of appreciating them or offering a suggestion to help ease their workload. Take the initiative whenever you can.

3. Make It Personal: Here's a bit of a catch – generic 'extras' don't always work. They might work once or twice, but not every time. so, try to really observe and adjust and tailor your efforts accordingly. People value receiving things they prefer and like.

4. Enjoy the Process: Lastly, and most importantly, creating wow moments should be a rewarding experience, not an exhausting and burdensome one. Approach this with curiosity of 'How can I make someone's day better?' and joy of 'I really made their day better!'

Pro-tip: A little extra effort — whether in attention, care, or thoughtfulness — turns the ordinary into the extraordinary and makes you unforgettable.

The Risk of Being Taken for Granted

As said earlier, the world is a harsh place to be in – so, there might be people who expect 'extra care' and small gestures without showing appreciation. Well, we can't toss this worry aside, this is an actual worry. But this shouldn't deter you from creating such moments. Consider nurses at hospitals who go out of their way to take care of their patients. Consider nurses who instead of just administering treatment and moving on, take their time to learn about their patients and converse with them regarding their patients' favorite things. It feels like a really small, simple act, but it makes a huge difference to someone who is stuck on a hospital stretcher, attached to IVs and feels isolated all the time. The other people in their surroundings may not fully understand and appreciate those nurses' actions, but those nurses will be remembered for a long time by their patients.

More importantly, your personal brand is built on your reputation and consistency. A single wow moment is memorable, but a reputation for consistently exceeding expectations sets you apart as someone trustworthy, reliable, and indispensable.

If you ever feel underappreciated, remind yourself that your efforts are planting seeds. The right people — bosses, clients, mentors, and peers — will recognize and reward your dedication in the long run.

Pro-tip: Be consistent in delivering wow moments, and be patient in seeing your efforts come to fruition.

The Influence of Wow

Influence isn't just about persuasion; it's about making a lasting impression. All the wow moments you create allow others to see in you a positive light. You become their friend, their mentor, their advisor, and their go-to person to talk to – and people do that rather instinctively.

Your wow moments might have helped others, but in the long run, they have shaped – or reshaped – your future. Opportunities come to those who stand out, and the best way to stand out is to deliver value beyond what's expected. Is having a "wow" mindset a part of your brand? If not, it should be. Influence comes to those who are memorable, who make people around them say "wow" on a consistent basis.

Practical Takeaways

- ✓ The world can feel increasingly negative, but small acts of kindness can break through the noise and leave a lasting impact.

- ✓ The *Art of Wow* is about exceeding expectations and adding personal touches that make interactions memorable.

- ✓ Simple gestures—like remembering someone's name, offering thoughtful assistance, or personalizing an experience—can have a big impact.

✓ Developing a *Wow Mindset* means paying attention to details, anticipating needs, personalizing interactions, and enjoying the process of creating positive experiences.

✓ Some may take extra effort for granted, but consistency in delivering wow moments will build a strong personal brand and create long-term benefits.

✓ Influence comes from being memorable and trusted, and the *Art of Wow* helps establish that trust and influence over time.

Exercises

➢ Reflect on a Wow Moment: Think of a time when someone went out of their way to surprise or impress you. Write down how it made you feel and why it stood out.

➢ Create Your Own Wow Plan: Identify three opportunities in your personal or professional life where you can exceed expectations this week. List specific actions you can take.

➢ Role Reversal Exercise: Imagine you are a customer, client, or coworker interacting with yourself. What wow moments would impress you? How can you incorporate these into your daily interactions?

➢ Gratitude Letter: Write a short letter or email to someone who has created a wow moment for you, expressing appreciation for their effort. Notice how this act of gratitude influences both them and yourself.

Chapter 5
Proverb #4 – Say Yes When You Get the Chance

I want you to ask yourself a few questions: Am I creating value for others and myself? Am I doing things that leave a lasting impact? And when people think of me, what will they remember? Tell yourself honestly, and you will quite frankly know what you need to do in life and what's stopping you from doing your best. We are stuck somewhere in the middle of 'not being exceptional' and 'not being average – we are just comfortable. Comfortable enough to get by, but not too keen to stand out. And quite comfortably, we risk being forgettable. Well, here is the thing about 'being forgettable', people forget you when something exceptional comes up. They forget to invite you, they forget to tell you of the golden opportunity, and they forget your accomplishment.

I know, a few of you reading this might think, 'Well, that's how introverted, shy, and socially anxious people are. We don't like being seen." This is going to sound a little harsh, but shyness might be the reason you are stuck somewhere unpleasant – in fact, nowhere. See, here's the thing, there are no rewards for invisibility. You don't have to be the loudest person in the room, but you have to be visible – visible enough to be heard, seen, and valued. If you hold back – by choice – and continue doing so, knowing your potential, you're allowing the world to trample right over you, and leave you neglected under that invisibility cloak. So, remind yourself, don't let the world overlook your value. And if you can relate to this, ask yourself, how long are you willing to stay unseen?

I wrote all this because I understand a lot of people face this, and don't want this to be discussed over and over again. It makes them uncomfortable. But this is just some advice, I hope you take it. Also, I addressed this here because this very chapter talks about seeking opportunities, making the best of those opportunities, and saying 'yes' every chance you get.

A little secret, saying 'yes' is often attributed to 'not-so-shy' people. So, try to be among those 'not-so-shy' people. Let's get to the point, shall we?

There are moments in life when an opportunity presents itself, and your first instinct is to hesitate. Maybe it's a new project, a promotion, or even an unexpected request that feels bigger than your current abilities. Your gut reaction? "I don't think I'm ready for this." It's natural to hesitate, we are unsure about the circumstances, we have doubts about the change, uncertainties scare us. And it's okay to feel that way – it's okay to behave like a human to such an unexpected opportunity. No one can take away the humanness of your behavior. But here's the thing—rarely do we ever feel 100% ready for something that pushes us beyond our comfort zone. Yes, comfort zone – the invisible fence that keeps safe, and keeps us small. It constantly reminds us, "It's safe here, it's easy here" and "It's familiar here." But progress never happens in easy, familiar, and safe. People who intend to change, progress, succeed are far, far, far out of their comfort zones. And those are the people who almost always step forward to grab every opportunity. So, don't ask yourself, "Am I ready?" instead ask, "Am I willing?"

A 2005 study by the Center for Creative Leadership, a world renowned leadership research firm surveyed 1,000 CEOs from large companies with a simple question: "Where did you learn to be a CEO?" The question might sound silly to most people. But the overwhelming response — 90% of them — was some variation of "When I was asked to do something that I had no idea how to do." One CEO described the moment as, "When I was an HR executive and was asked to lead IT." Another said, "When I spent my career in Marketing and was asked to lead HR." These stories highlight an important truth: transformative growth happens when you step out of the known, and into the unknown – stretching your skills and forcing yourself to learn on the fly. Saying 'yes' to challenges you're not fully prepared for is often the very thing that prepares you to succeed.

Saying 'yes' when the right opportunity arises can be one of the most powerful decisions you make. It can be the only decision that sets you on the path to achieve your goals. It's often the difference between staying stagnant and experiencing real, meaningful growth.

I assure you of this because I know this firsthand.

Pro-tip: Opportunities find those who step forward – you make sure you're seen, heard, and valued.

My 'Yes' That Changed Everything

Years ago, I was working in a comfortable role, doing work I knew inside and out. Every day was 'just another day' with almost similar tasks and assignments. Somewhere I knew I needed something new, something exciting, and something that wasn't what I was doing at that time. Well, my silent wish was heard. One day, my boss approached me with an opportunity — leading a high-profile project that was way outside my wheelhouse. My first thoughts? *This is so out of my depth. What if I fail? What if they realize I'm not as capable as they think? I should stick to what I know.*

But then I realized I was stuck in my job; I was resisting change and possibly progress. I was too comfortable to leave the familiarities – and that would bar me from my success. So, instead of saying no, I took a deep breath and said, "Yes. I'll do it."

That one decision changed my entire career trajectory. I had to learn on the fly, ask for help, and stretch myself in ways I never had before. It was uncomfortable, sometimes quite tough, and demanding. But by the end of it, I had built stronger relationships, developed new skills, and gained confidence in my ability to take on challenges. Most importantly, I have built an unshakable trust in myself. I knew then challenges don't scare me, it's just me scaring myself from challenges. Every challenge, when tackled with attention, strategy, and right execution, becomes a rewarding experience. So, the next time you face a challenge, ask yourself, "Am I unqualified? Or am I just scared?"

Lastly, I also realized that no one ever really 'feels ready.' Growth happens in the stretch. In uncertainties, I discovered my true capability and capacity. To be honest, how can you be ready when you haven't experienced anything beyond comfortable and familiar? So, quit waiting for some miraculous readiness, and start saying 'yes' every chance you get.

Pro-tip: Growth doesn't come from feeling ready
– it comes from taking a leap.

Your Unique Skills Make You Ready

Here's a truth you need to hear: You are never truly unqualified for an opportunity that presents itself. We tend to overthink, we think of our failures, our mistakes, and all the mishaps that happened, label ourselves as 'incapable' and decline a wonderful opportunity. That's typically what most people do. Except you must tell yourself that you bring a unique set of skills, experiences, and perspectives that no one else has. Everyone is unique, undoubtedly, and everyone has the right to their perspectives. No two people ever solve a challenge similarly. So, don't fret about being incapable, you're just you – uniquely you.

At first, the challenge may feel unfamiliar, but the qualities that got you where you are today — be it your problem-solving ability, adaptability, communication skills — are timeless and transferable. Noone can take those away from you. They are yours!

When a new challenge arises, don't focus on what you lack. Instead, shift your mindset to: What do I already bring to the table that can help me succeed? In fact, go on and list the qualifications and skills you have against what is required to tackle the challenge. Believe me, you'll end up having more skills needed to tackle that challenge. And if you fall short of skills, remind yourself that life is a long journey of learning new things, not fearing new things. This simple perspective change can turn fear into confidence.

Let me share a story of a very successful large company I worked for in the late 90s. This company showed me the value of this proverb. Every 2 years, the executive team would gather in a room and basically "take the job of the person to your right." Yes, you read this right; every executive got the job of the person sitting on their right side. Each executive took on an area that was new to them and they said yes! The last two CEOs at this company managed five different departments over their career, preparing them to be a CEO. They said yes and it increased their influence and career trajectory. Not only did they get to experience the roles of different people, they built a skillset they couldn't have otherwise.

Pro-tip: You're more capable than you think –
take every chance to grow and learn.

Saying Yes Without Overloading Yourself

Let's be clear—this isn't about saying yes to everything and burning yourself out. Burning out will only make you despise whatever you are doing and take you further away from progress. There's a big difference between stepping up to meaningful challenges and taking on every single task thrown your way. You're not supposed to finish someone else's unfinished tasks, or answer in their place. The key is to say yes to the things that align with your goals, your core responsibilities, and the bigger picture of where you want to go. Say yes to opportunities, not every request and favor. A little bit of help and favor never harmed anyone, but doing it to a point of exhausting yourself is senseless. Don't become a doormat, don't become an 'easily available for every favor' person. You are responsible for your progress and 'staying stuck' situation. So, don't let anyone else dictate it for you.

Say yes strategically, and by that, I mean:

- Identify opportunities that help you grow.

- Recognize when a challenge aligns with your strengths.

- Being willing to stretch without drowning yourself in commitments.

If an opportunity feels overwhelming, ask yourself, 'Does this push me in the direction I want to grow?' If the answer is yes, then lean in. If the answer is no, quit it immediately.

Pro-tip: Say yes to growth, not burn-out. Focus on opportunities, not on favors.

Overcoming Fear: They Believe in You

Look, I know, it isn't as easy as it seems, and I understand your hesitation. But fear is natural when stepping into the unknown. No one likes uncertainties and unfamiliarity, but hey, it's only an unfamiliarity until we get to experience it. Trust me, once you peel off from the comfortable, you will never want to retreat to it. The unknown, the unfamiliar will become your new reality – and you will learn to adapt, adopt, and adjust accordingly.

Remind yourself — if someone is offering you an opportunity, it's because they believe in you! They see something in you that you might not even see in yourself yet. Your comfort zone blindsided you from all the hidden gems in you.

"The universe buries strange jewels deep within us all, and then stands back to see if we can find them. The hunt to discover those jewels––that's creative living."

— *Elizabeth Gilbert, Big Magic: Creative living Beyond Fear.*

That one step, that single decision, that one opportunity might keep you sleepless for a few nights – but can change the entire course of your life. The discomfort of trying something unfamiliar will last a few days, but the regret of losing that chance will last a lifetime. So, ask yourself, 'Will you let fear hold you back? Or will you take the chance and see what lies on the other side?' Also, just so you know, companies don't hand out big responsibilities for fun; they do it because they trust you can handle it. Your willingness to take risks and say yes can build that trust even further, opening even more doors.

In my life, I have been asked to do some crazy things. While being an HR executive, I was asked to lead the packaging and warehouse function for our company. I said "yes" and it was one of the greatest experiences of my career! When I was an HR executive for an equipment company, they asked me to hit the road and be a regional sales manager. I said "yes" and I probably got the equivalent of an MBA in those six months. So, let your experiences be your teacher sometimes.

Pro-tip: Fear thrives in inaction. Growth thrives in motion, not in overthinking.

Knowing When to Say No

Of course, there are times when the right answer is no. Not every opportunity is the right one, and sometimes, saying yes can mean spreading yourself too thin. Recognizing when to decline is just as important as knowing when to say yes.

Say no when:

- The opportunity doesn't align with your long-term goals.

- You're already at full capacity and can't give it your best effort.

- It takes away from the things that truly matter in your career or personal life.

The next time you're faced with an apparently 'scary' opportunity, pause and think – don't overthink. Instead of immediately doubting yourself, ask, 'What could saying yes to this lead to?' More often than not, the biggest breakthroughs come from the moments when we take a deep breath and go for it.

Say yes when you get the chance. You never know where it might take you. So, let's go back to our brand—is your brand typified by you saying "yes" and diving into new opportunities? Hopefully this chapter has convinced you that saying yes to things can increase your influence dramatically. Give it a try today!!

Pro-tip: Saying yes opens doors, but knowing when to say no keeps you aligned with your goals.

Practical Takeaways

- ✓ Growth happens when you say yes to challenges that push you beyond your comfort zone.

- ✓ You are more prepared than you think—focus on your strengths and transferable skills.

- ✓ Saying yes strategically means aligning opportunities with your goals, not overloading yourself.

- ✓ Fear is natural, but remember that if someone offers you an opportunity, they believe in your potential.

- ✓ Knowing when to say no is just as important as knowing when to say yes—prioritize wisely.

✓ Every 'yes' has the potential to open doors to bigger and better opportunities.

Exercises

➢ Reflect on a Past 'Yes': Think about a time when you said yes to an opportunity that initially felt overwhelming. Write down what happened, how you handled it, and what you learned from the experience.

➢ Identify Transferable Skills: List five skills you have that can be applied to various situations. Next time you're faced with a new challenge, revisit this list and see how your existing strengths can help you succeed.

➢ Practice Saying 'No': Write down three situations where saying 'no' would have been the right choice. Reflect on how you can make better decisions in the future to avoid overcommitting.

➢ Take a Small Risk This Week: Challenge yourself to say 'yes' to something outside your comfort zone, whether it's volunteering for a new project at work, attending a networking event, or trying a new skill. Write about how it went and what you learned.

Chapter 6
Proverb #5 – Adopt a mindset that You Are Never Wasting Time

Ever felt like you are trapped? Like you want to escape but you can't find your way out. A trap that suffocates you mentally, and even without arduous physical labor, you feel physically drained, too. You keep telling yourself every day that you don't want to do this, but you do it regardless.

You wake up dreading the day ahead – the moment you wake up, you despise yourself and this trap. You're stuck in a cycle of monotony, questioning how you got here in the first place. you recall that it wasn't this bad in the beginning, so how did it get this bad? You prepare for the day, consciously aware that you need to get rid of this trap. You work in this trap for most of your day, each passing second there tests your every ounce of single, and every single day your patience hangs by the thinnest fiber. Every day when the clock strikes 5 or 6 PM, you are released and relieved, only to start this all over again. You return to your abode, promising yourself that you will soon find the way out. And you hope for a respite and release from the trap.

Relatable much? Yes, we have all experienced – only a few are lucky enough to never experience this 'trap-like' feeling. So, what makes your crappy job a trap? Maybe it is fear of the unknown, financial obligations, or simply not knowing what comes next.

Whatever the reason, the feeling of entrapment is real, and it wears on you. It tests you and keeps testing you until either you snap or the entrapment releases you.

But here's the bitter truth: The trap isn't just the job itself – it's the way we perceive it. When we feel powerless, our circumstances seem immovable. But when we recognize that every situation, no matter how frustrating, holds an opportunity, we begin to regain control. The escape isn't always quitting; sometimes, it's shifting how we approach our work, extracting lessons, and using them as stepping stones to something greater. I know you must be saying, "Oh, you don't know how being stuck in a crappy job feels like." I do, I really know what a crappy job is, but I am encouraging you to learn lessons from these jobs. I have picked rocks in farm fields, picked weeds on my hands and knees in a garden as long as a football field, dug ditches all summer long for the telephone company, baled hay in the hot summer sun, shoveled snow before my Dad could afford a snowblower. These are all crappy jobs – and they will be regarded as crappy jobs, I guess, until the end of times. But did I whine and complain because I had all the reason to? I probably did!! But influence comes when we realize that whining and complaining take you nowhere. It is in that mindset change that I learned the invaluable lesson of self-esteem from accomplishing such a task, the value of muscles that are sore at the end of the day. Also, in those roles, I learned the value of safety and caring for the people who work around you, how to treat customers who are sometimes not happy with you, how to deal with co-workers who are not like you at all. How to handle conflict, how to solve problems, how to run equipment and tools, were only a few of skills and lessons I garnered through these crappy jobs. I don't want to go back and do these jobs again – but I am thankful for the life lessons learned in the middle of "the suck". And I will forever cherish the humility these jobs instilled in me. Noone can take these hard-earned lessons away from me. They are mine.

More than changing the job itself, it is our mindset that needs a shift – a dramatic change. We only consider jobs that give us fancy cars, expensive insurances, and spacious offices of value – anything below this is downright crappy. No doubt, all the fancy corporate jobs improve our lifestyles to an extent, but believe me, even there people aren't satisfied with what they have. Focus on the improvement of skills and betterment in your character, a job offers before expecting a six-figure job for yourself. Also, you need to be someone who adds value wherever they are, before becoming someone 'valuable.'

Pro-tip: Reframe your mindset. Gain skills. Add value. Outgrow the trap instead of just escaping it.

A Shift in Mindset

In the movie Elf, when Buddy's dad finally had to have some time free of Buddy, he sent him to the mailroom. The movie portrayed the mailroom as a monotonous environment with not a lot of joyful employees. Buddy, employing his inquisitive style, childish abandon, and naïve view of the world, turned the mailroom into an atmosphere of fun, laughter and levity. Now, they weren't getting much done during that scene, but take a nugget of wisdom from Buddy. Many of us have been "sent to the mailroom". We have had jobs that we didn't want to do. To me, it's all about mindset.

We keep hating our job, despising ourselves, and keep waiting for something better, without even trying to add value or learn a few more things and lessons from the job. And that's exactly where we go miserably wrong. The reality is that every experience — no matter how unappealing — has something to teach you. Those who recognize this truth will find themselves better prepared for future success. The right mindset is not "I'm stuck here." Instead, it's "What can I take from this experience?" This small shift in thinking changes everything. Even in the most mundane roles, you can develop valuable skills, build resilience, and gain insights that will serve you later in life.

Let me explain this with an experience I had not long ago. I met Monica, who was assigned to be the helper at a self-checkout line at a mega grocery chain's store near me in Phoenix. I am sure Monica is used to seeing thousands of customers each day. There was nothing special about me. but when I needed help at the checkout station, she approached me with a greeting I would love to get every day on my way out the door. She really cared about what she was doing. She joked with me, helped me perfectly, and even entered in her code, so I could get a discount as a frequent shopper. Monica made me feel like I was the only shopper she helped that day. I'm not sure if she loved her job or not, but to me, she seemed like the happiest person on the planet. She chooses to add value where she is planted, to learn what she can from every situation. Whatever job you have, be the absolute best at it.

Pro-tip: Shift your mindset — every job offers opportunities to learn and grow.

Lessons from the Trenches

I know this because I've lived it. I've had jobs that tested my patience, self-worth, and stamina. More recently, I can distinctly remember in 2001 being given the task of renegotiating the union contract at our company. I remember how lost I was, how much I was a "fish out of water". It's scary not knowing anything about the topic you have been assigned to. I had a great mentor that was there for me, but still, this was an unlikely role for me. I remember how hard it was, how much effort it took, and good grief, I made mistakes, plenty of them. At the end of the day, we did renegotiate the contract and continued to have good relations with our workforce. I do remember learning so much from that experience. At the time, when reassigned, I do remember that period of uncertainty and steep learning was behind me. However, 24 years later, I am now in the same position I was in 2001. Now, people lean on me for union relations, finding effective labor policies that benefit all, and renegotiating our union contracts. Looking back, I'm grateful for those early experiences and lessons that shaped me 24years later. So, ladies and gentlemen, no matter what you are doing, you are not wasting time. You are learning something today. Even though it seems to suck today, trust me, it will benefit you in your future. Call me when you find this to be true in your life. It has been true in my life and lives of hundreds of people I have seen through the years.

Frustration is Inevitable—Growth is a Choice

Let me state the most controversial things you have ever heard, frustration is a gift. See, I am not only one saying this.

"Frustration, although quite painful at times, is a very positive and essential part of success."

– Bo Bennett

Yep, you read that right, frustrations might be the fuel driving you to your success. It signals that you're pushing boundaries, that you care, and that growth is just beyond the discomfort. The key isn't to avoid frustration but to harness it. So, it's normal to feel frustrated when you have an 'undesirable' job. But the key to overcoming it lies in reframing the situation. Instead of thinking, "I am wasting time here," shift to "I am building something valuable." The skills, habits, and work ethic you develop will pay off in ways you can't yet see. Also, please be in no rush of seeing your efforts' fruits – the sweetest fruit takes the longest to grow and ripen. I know it's like adding oil to the fire – asking you to be patient when you're struggling with frustration. See, every highly successful person has a story about a tough job that shaped them. Think of your patience and frustration as the time of 'being prepared' for your best self.

From CEOs who once mopped floors to entrepreneurs who worked endless hours in thankless positions, they all credit those experiences as foundational to their success. The difference? They didn't let their circumstances define their attitude. And they didn't call those mundane and crappy jobs 'sucky' ones.

No job is beneath you if you treat it as a learning experience, if you think of it as a stepping stone rather than a dead end. Whether it's learning patience, refining communication skills, or simply proving to yourself that you can endure hardship, every job adds something to your personal and professional toolkit.

So, if you find yourself in a job you don't love, ask yourself: "What can I take from this?" When you adopt the mindset that every experience has value, you will always be growing—and that is how you set yourself up for greater opportunities ahead. You only need to choose to look at things differently. Creating the capacity to influence others means changing our mindset about where we are currently planted. High influence people adopt a mindset that are never wasting time. They learn and grow, even in "the suck". When it comes to your brand, and your ability to build trust and influence others, those who apply this proverb, and come out of crappy jobs with new skills, will have a mindset that will stand the test of time. Call me when you learn this lesson yourself. Because you will!

Pro-tip: Success comes from pushing through challenges and frustrations, not avoiding them.

Practical Takeaways

- ✓ The way you approach a job shapes what you gain from it. A shift from resentment to curiosity can transform your experience.
- ✓ Recognizing that frustration often stems from perception allows you to reclaim control and find meaning in any role.
- ✓ Hard work, teamwork, problem-solving, and resilience are skills that carry over into future success.
- ✓ Even if a job feels like a dead end, the skills you build will serve you in unexpected ways.
- ✓ No job is a waste if you extract lessons from it. Each experience adds to your personal and professional growth.

Exercises

- ➢ Reframe Your Experience: Write down the most frustrating aspects of your current or past "crappy job." Now, for each one, find a positive takeaway or skill you developed from it. Example: "Dealing with rude customers" → "Improved patience and conflict resolution skills."

➤ Identify Hidden Skills: List five skills you gained from an unappealing job. How can you apply them to your current or future career?

➤ Mindset Challenge: For one week, consciously shift your mindset at work. Instead of focusing on what you dislike, look for opportunities to learn, grow, or help others. Journal about the differences you notice in your attitude and experience.

➤ Role Model Research: Research a successful person who once worked a tough or menial job. Write down the lessons they learned from that experience and how they applied them to their success.

➤ Gratitude Shift: Each day, write down one thing you are grateful for in your current job — no matter how small. This practice will help you see value where you once saw frustration.

Chapter 7
Proverb #6 – Develop a Giver Mindset

"You can have everything in life you want, if you will just help other people get what they want." — *Zig Ziglar*

Today, we are all in an endless spiral of 'wish lists', what we want to have, what we want to achieve, what we want others to do for us. Our conversations, ambitions, and even relationships often revolve around "getting" more: more recognition, more success, more comfort, more validation. But in this pursuit, we often forget that the most fulfilled lives aren't built by constant receiving—they're built by consistent contribution.

I do believe that several years back, there was no concept as 'faith in humanity restored' – I mean how absurd that is. When did we lose our faith in humanity and why? When did humanity, collectively, stoop so low that it needed something as basic as helping someone to restore people's faith in it? Quite frankly, the world has witnessed humanity murder, bombs, oppression, massacres, stealing, and what not, for far too long. If you don't believe me, just switch to any news channel, and you will see at least four or five headlines related to the prevalent evils. And again, even if something good happens, it becomes a piece of news. Doing something, basically a human becomes news.

Well, where does it all stem from? When someone decides they need to *take* lives to satisfy their political and beastly motives; when some lunatic believes that the world has *taken* far too much from him, so he plans on *taking* away lives he didn't own; when someone thinks they are racially superior and their race should *take* over the world. It's all deeply wired in a mindset of taking—where self-interest overshadows service, and giving has become the exception rather than the norm. When kindness becomes newsworthy, it's a sign that generosity has become rare—when in truth, it should be our baseline, not our headline.

The world needs to contribute to it, humanity needs its humans to at least act like humans – it's all the game of mindset. And when mindsets change, miracles happen. When we shift from a mindset of scarcity to one of generosity, something profound happens: we stop chasing and start creating. We stop chasing pointless motives, we give up on harmful agendas, and we shun all the beliefs that lead us astray from contributing more and doing better. We begin to see opportunities to give—our time, our encouragement, our effort, our presence. In doing so, we not only enrich others but elevate ourselves. The irony is that when we give freely, without keeping score, we often receive far more than we ever imagined. Not always in material form, but in meaning, connection, and impact. The world doesn't need more takers. It needs more givers—people willing to sow seeds, not just collect fruit.

In my 40 years in the work world and my 60 plus years of life, I have come to the believe that people get up on one side of the bed or the other every morning. They either get up on the side of the bed and have the attitude of "I can't wait to tackle the day. I am looking for opportunities to pour into others, bring encouragement, growth, development, support to those around me." Let's call this the Giver side of the bed. Or they get up on the side of the bed that says, "I can't wait to tackle the day. I'm going to look for opportunities to get ahead today, to look for ways to get my share, to save my emotions for efforts that benefit me. To get all the world has coming to me today." Let's call that side of the bed, the Taker side.

In my experience, you are either a Giver or a Taker. I have heard others say, 'You are either a sprinkler or you are a drain.' A sprinkler spreads their life, giving water as far and wide as they can. A drain, however, takes from everything around, bringing it to themselves.

It's a simple idea, but one that holds incredible power.

Givers and Takers walk the same hallways, sit in the same meetings, attend the same social events, and work on the same teams — but they leave completely different impressions. One builds bridges; the other burns energy. One inspires growth; the other stifles progress. One plants seeds of trust; the other pulls from others' roots without ever watering the soil.

The question is: which one are you becoming?

Pro-tip: Begin each day with this question:
"What can I give today? A Giver mindset
multiplies your impact, influence, and inner
fulfillment.

75

The Daily Choice That Shapes Your Influence

Let me repeat myself, your mindset dictates your behavior. The Giver mindset doesn't limit you to what you do—it's mostly about how you show up. It's a lens you choose to see through, a rhythm you choose to move in. Here is how I can help you understand this. In the Greek language, the terms 'em and en' mean 'to give power' or 'to cover with'. So, whenever you come across words like 'empower' and 'encourage' we understand they mean 'to give power or 'to give courage'. Or the word 'embrace' means to 'give brace or hold someone up'. So, someone with a giver mindset will lead an Em/En kind of life. They pour into others, and they always wake up on the Em/En side of the bed every morning.

Think of someone right now that you love to be around. What are their attributes? Do you find yourself using some Ems and some Ens? Do they encourage, empower, entrust, enlist, and enable? If so, do we want to be like these people? Do we emulate them? Contrast that with people who suck your energy. They talk about themselves, they steal your joy, take credit for accomplishments that may have even been yours? In 1989, I saw this contrast in someone close to me. He worked for a boss who was all about sales, how he looked to his boss, what we could get from our customers, how we could build his own sales stockpile, and a whole lot of other sales gibberish. My friend, who was not wired that way at all, was frustrated, had low self-esteem, and was threatened to be fired almost every day due to his lack of "buying in" to the aggressive approach. His boss was a taker, sucking the energy out of everyone around him. Ultimately, my friend lost his job under this manager. As it turns out, it was one of the best things that ever happened to him. In his next role, he worked for a Giver. His next boss was a master at the Em and the En. He gave encouragement, empowerment, enablement, and support. My friend's performance skyrocketed. Sales, relationships, leads, results all went through the roof. Choosing to be a Giver yields dividends, increases results, and improves relationships. Tomorrow, when you throw your legs over the side of the bed, decide to be a Giver. A Giver empowers. A Taker extracts.

When you interact with people, they can feel your energy before you speak a word. When you operate with a Giver mindset, people feel seen, supported, and uplifted in your presence. Just your presence – you don't even have to give a speech for motivating them. But when you slip into a Taker mindset, even unintentionally, people often feel used, diminished, or dismissed. Take a good look around yourself, and ask yourself, which energy are you spreading?

Pro-tip: Be the person who Energizes, Empower, Encourage, Embrace, and Enable others, not the one who drains them.

What Makes A Giver

Let's try to picture this through the example of 'Sprinkler vs Drain'. We all have seen sprinklers around us, in gardens, in parks, or maybe in stadiums. Sprinklers bring life to everything around them. They distribute water, in this case, say, energy, creating lush growth wherever they reach. Drains, on the other hand, suck everything toward themselves. They focus on themselves, pulling everything towards them, but their impact often invisible — until you realize you're just exhausted from being around them. And believe me when I say this, one doesn't have to spend decades to sense the energies. People can sense who's watering the room and who's draining it just by a single meeting. And make no mistake: people feel it even before they can name it. The energy you radiate suffices to determine if you are a giver or a taker.

Still, if you are unaware in which category you lie, here is how you can distinguish. Let's make this practical. Givers show up every day in ways:

- They ask *"How can I help?"* instead of *"What can I get?"*

- They listen to understand, not just to reply.

- They celebrate others' wins without feeling threatened.

- They offer credit generously and take responsibility willingly.

- They encourage, support, and speak life into others — even when it costs them nothing.

- They contribute ideas without needing the spotlight.

- They elevate others without lowering themselves.

However, Takers, on the contrary, present themselves as,

- They ask "What's in it for me?" instead of "How can I help?"
- They listen to respond — or to redirect the spotlight — rather than to truly understand.
- They feel threatened by others' success and compete instead of celebrating.
- They take credit quickly and shift blame even faster.
- They rarely encourage unless it benefits them or boosts their image.
- They share ideas only when recognition is guaranteed.
- They push others down or aside to lift themselves.

You don't have to speak the loudest or be forceful to get yourself noticed – you can simply give value, build trust, and light the way forward for others.

Pro-tip: Choose to uplift, not absorb; to energize, not deplete. Your presence should leave people better, not bitter.

The Myth: Givers Finish Last

One of the biggest misconceptions about a Giver mindset is the fear of being taken advantage of. People may presume you're available almost every time and any time. So, you might end up losing more than gaining anything at all.

But here's the truth: Givers don't finish last — over-givers do. It's not about being a martyr or giving until you're empty. It's about choosing generosity, a commitment to contribution over consumption – consumption that plagues us today.

We need to know the difference between being generous and being a doormat. Healthy Givers know their boundaries. They give from a full cup, not an empty one. They serve with wisdom, not risk their dignity or well-being. And because they build a reputation of integrity, service, and trust, Givers often rise to the top. There aren't people who follow those who suck energy and know how to take, people follow Givers – by choice, not because they have to.

Imagine walking into a room where everyone is trying to get something. Now imagine walking into a room where everyone is trying to give something.

Which room would you choose to be in?

Now, imagine you are the reason that second room exists. How? Because your habit of giving turned people into Givers. That's the power of the Giver mindset. When you model it, you don't just influence people — you build and improve the culture around you. You become a multiplier of value, and a person others naturally trust. And in a world, that's constantly taking, be the light for others, be the Giver.

I read this proverb and it has stuck with me: you don't lose by lifting others — you grow.

The Giver mindset doesn't take you away from your success; it multiplies it. It attracts allies, builds loyalty, and earns trust — the real currency of influence.

Choose to be the kind of person who adds value wherever you go. The world needs more of that kind of energy.

And when you wake up tomorrow, make a deliberate choice of waking up on the right side of the bed.

Choose the Giver side of the bed. You will find your influence growing when you choose a Giver mindset...promise.

Pro-tip: Givers thrive when they give from a
place of strength, not sacrifice.

Practical Takeaways

- ✓ Your attitude is a decision, not a personality trait. Start each day intentionally by choosing to add value rather than extract it.
- ✓ Givers bring life, trust, and momentum to others. Takers sap energy and create friction. Your influence grows when others feel uplifted around you.
- ✓ The Giver mindset isn't about self-sacrifice; it's about strategic generosity. When you give wisely, you build loyalty, trust, and long-term success.
- ✓ Givers thrive when they give from fullness, not burnout. Protect your energy so you can keep contributing meaningfully.
- ✓ A compliment, a helping hand, a listening ear — all simple ways to live the Giver mindset every day. Influence starts with small, intentional choices.
- ✓ Your energy and attitude leave a lasting impression. When you operate as a Giver, you create a ripple effect that extends far beyond the moment.

Exercises

- ➢ Self-Reflection: Think about your recent interactions — at work, home, or in social settings. In what situations do I naturally operate as a Giver? Where do I find myself slipping into a Taker mindset? What impact does my energy have on the people around me? Write down two examples from the past week — one where you gave energy to others, and one where you might have unintentionally drained it.

➢ Identify Your "Sprinkler" Strengths: Every Giver has a unique style. What's yours? Are you an encourager? A problem-solver? A connector? A listener? A helper behind the scenes? List three personal strengths you can use to bring life to others this week.

➢ The Giver Challenge – 5 Days of Intentional Giving: For the next five days, commit to one act of intentional giving each day. It can be simple—but purposeful. At the end of the challenge, reflect: What changed in you? What changed in others?

➢ Gratitude Flip: Shift Your Focus: Givers often see what's right before they notice what's wrong. Let's train your perspective. List 5 things you're grateful for in your personal life. List 5 things you appreciate about people you work or live with. Now, tell at least two of those people what you appreciate about them today.

Chapter 8
Proverb #7 – Never Burn A Bridge

"You may encounter many defeats, but you must not be defeated. In fact, it may be necessary to encounter the defeats, so you can know who you are, what you can rise from, how you can still come out of it." — Maya Angelou

Recall your last moment of disappointment – when you felt like you'd been hit by a storm on a clear day. Recall that precise rush of emotions – the sudden sorrow, the murder of your anticipation, that frustration, and then perhaps, an outrage. Or an emotionally charged spew of words. While you may recall the disappointing and frustrating part quite well, the reactionary part is forgotten and disregarded, as it was just equally reactionary – and in your head justified. Justified or not, ask yourself, was it right? More importantly, what would people remember about you? I can assure you, they weren't aware of the frustration festering within you, but they witnessed the fire your mouth put around. So, what do they see you as now – rational and composed, or erratic and wild? I know a typical reaction to this question, "I don't care what others think, I did what felt right. I had to give 'em a piece of my mind." Well, you need to care, and this book is all about teaching you how to care about the right things because these things make or break your brand. So, here is your lesson on disappointment and how to handle it.

First, go read the quote again – or a few words from Maya Angelou if you like. To explain with an analogy, disappointment is like a sudden storm that catches you off guard on what seems like a clear day. One moment, you're walking confidently under blue skies—full of plans, hope, and momentum—and the next, the clouds roll in, the rain pours, and visibility disappears. You feel soaked, disoriented, and frustrated.

You can't control the storm—but you can control how you respond to it. You could shout at the sky, curse the weather, or give up and sit in the rain. Or you could pause, take cover, wait it out, and keep moving once it clears. Because the truth is, storms don't last forever. And if you're paying attention, they often leave behind fresh air, clearer skies, and a deeper appreciation for the clear, sunny days.

Disappointment doesn't define you—it reveals your character. It shows whether you react with panic or poise, whether you let the rain drown your spirit or choose to walk forward, wet but wiser.

As a Dad, I had the privilege of partnering with my wonderful wife of 35 years to parent three boys. We are so proud of them as they have grown into successful young men, with healthy careers, partners, families, and friends.

I can remember many times being proud of their accomplishments as they grew. As a parent, you remember the awards, the accomplishments, etc. Most recently, all three of our boys were named to their High School hall of fame for their accomplishments as a golf team in 2012. As you might expect, that was a proud moment for this Dad. However, I can honestly say, the proudest I have ever been of each of my boys was watching them navigate through disappointments.

Our oldest son PJ, announced to us one day that his dream was to be an FBI special agent. He made it through 9 months of tests, assessments, physical demands, mental testing, security clearances, etc. Out of the 10,000 applicants received by the FBI that year, 900 made the cut. PJ made it! As he prepared for the certainty of going to Quantico and living his dream, his wife announced that they were expecting their first child. Amidst excitement and planning for this life-changing event, PJ knew he had a huge decision to make. His excitement for a new baby was contrasted with the reality of knowing that he now had a huge decision to make. I watched him very closely during this time. I saw no sadness, no regrets. Instead, I saw leadership, trust, and thoughtfulness. So, through prayer, wise counsel, and contemplation, PJ and his wife decided to turn down the FBI opportunity, and focus his attention on his growing family. I am so proud of him for achieving a job offer from the FBI, but even prouder of him for making a tough, values-based decision to turn down the FBI and grow his family instead. Not long after this decision, he began a new job and is very happy with his decision. With now two of our grandbabies in his home at the time of this book, we are enjoying that part of his life along with him.

The truest test of character doesn't come in moments of triumph but in how we navigate disappointment. Anyone can smile when things are going their way. It's easy to be gracious when life is offering applause. But when the storms arrive, when things don't go as planned — that's when your real brand is revealed.

Disappointments are indeed painful, annoying interruptions to our plans but they are our defining moments. They offer a rare opportunity to shape how others perceive you, build trust, and influence people in more lasting ways than accomplishments ever could.

Why? Because people watch you more closely when you're in a season of disappointment than they do in a season of victory. They tune in to your tone, your body language, your words, and your choices. Your reaction becomes part of your story — the one people will tell others about and the one you tell yourself.

Pro-tip: Your grace under pressure is your greatest influence. Handle the storm; don't become it.

Your Brand is Loudest When Things Go Wrong

Think of a leader you admire. Chances are, your respect for them didn't come just from their victories — but from how they carried themselves through tough times. Disappointments are like highlighters: they reveal what's already inside. A person who reacts with grace, calm, and perspective inspires others and leaves a lasting impression.

Now think of someone opposite — someone who fires off a rage-filled email, lashes out at colleagues, or spirals into blame. Or worse, even threaten others with consequences. Let me just take a moment to tell you why there are people who are almost always inclined to such a reaction - it makes them feel powerful. You have the power to threaten others, or now you have the power to 'not care', or now you have the power to not behave in a certain way. All that sense of false power at the cost of permanently staining your credibility. In business, leadership, or personal life, people remember how you handle loss, rejection, or failure more than the fact that you experienced it. Trust me, people will forget about your frustration the next moment you tell them about it. But how you carried it will be a tale to tell.

Pro-tip: In moments of disappointment, power isn't in how loudly you react — but in how wisely you respond.

Grace in the Gap: Where Influence Grows

Here is a not-so-known fact, your reactions make people feel safe or unsafe, respected or disrespected, and inspired or demotivated. Again, I have another story to share – and this time of my second son. Our middle son RJ, when he was in 8th grade, earned his way onto the state tournament golf team at his high school. At the time, an 8th grader was a rare sight on a varsity golf team. During the final round of his competition, RJ learned and taught a lesson in disappointment that I will never forget – and believe people watching and his competitors remember it too. The round was mainly uneventful with RJ playing well. He was 6 over par as he reached the 11th hole. The 11th was eventful. RJ's drive went into some long grass next to the green and required a bit of a search for his ball among that tall grass. Having found what was identified as his ball, RJ completed the hole without incident. Teeing off on the 12th tee box, RJ put a nice drive in play and started to walk back to his bag to put his driver away. As he did that, I could see him looking at his bag, pacing back and forth, looking to the sky, and was in obvious distress. Shortly after that, he took his glove off and gathered his playing partners on the tee box with him. As they were gathered, RJ took off his hat and shook the hands of his playing competitors. Anyone who knows the game of golf knows that when a player takes off his/her hat, it is a respectful sign that win or lose, their day is done. It is a sign of respect and honor for your competitors. RJ forfeited his final round and disqualified himself from the competition. As it turned out, even though the ball found on #11 was the exact brand and number as the ball RJ was playing, it was NOT his ball. After putting that wrong ball "in play" on #12, he realized what happened. No one except him knew. He could have gone forward and finished his round with not a soul in the world knowing what happened. Instead, RJ admitted the rule infraction and disqualified himself from the competition. He was immensely disappointed. But he held his head high, walked along with his teammates, and cheered them to the finish line. The pride I felt in that moment still brings me to tears today as I write this story. It was a hard lesson to learn, but one that positively impacted him and those around him. The Director of the state HS athletic department sought me out after the round to compliment me on RJ's actions. As a Sophomore and a Senior, RJ won a state individual title in both years and went on to a successful collegiate golf career.

True influencers aren't just those who win the deal, get the promotion, win the championship, or seal the sale. They're the ones who can take a setback and still make people feel safe, respected, and inspired. See, your disappointments won't last, that gutted feeling will fade but your reaction will echo far louder and far longer. That is what people will remember, and that is what defines your brand.

When you keep your composure, even when you're disappointed, you send a signal:

- I'm emotionally mature.

- I care about relationships more than my fragile ego.

- I can be trusted in difficult times.

That signal builds trust. And trust builds influence. Your choice – to act wisely or to react loudly.

Pro-tip: People don't just watch how you win — they remember how you lose. Let your setbacks speak of strength, not spite.

What Happens When You React Impulsively

Of course, disappointments are frustrating. You worked hard. You expected a result. You feel let down. All those emotions are real and justified in that moment. But don't let that moment destroy the brand you've been building. Your reaction doesn't have to be destructive. Be calm, and realize you are being watched very closely. If you watch basketball, you know when a referee calls a foul on a player, they watch their reaction, they stare them down. If the player does anything out of line, a technical foul is on the way. In the same way, try not to be so dramatic. Yeah, drastically dramatic is the usual reaction to disappointment.

Okay, the last "Dad brag" I have is about our youngest son CJ. He was a recruiter for a very well-respected recruiting firm. Having worked three successful years as a recruiter, he applied for a promotion. He was so excited. It was the culmination of his work thus far and he knew he had a great chance at it. He made it through several interviews and made it to the final decision. He was so excited anticipating a possible promotion into an area he was dying to get into. The call came, the anticipation was high. He did not get the promotion. Distressed, disappointed, and frustrated were three of the primary emotions he was processing. I watched him closely as he navigated through it. Later that week, there was a happy hour to honor the person who did get the job. CJ attended the happy hour and gave the toast congratulating the person who was awarded the job. CJ's boss was standing next to the Sr. Director over the entire division while CJ was giving the toast. He leaned to CJ's boss and said, "This shows me everything I need to know about him." The book is about making choices that affect our perception, and our brand. At that moment, CJ's "brand" in the organization's mind was impacted greatly. Time will tell how it will pay off for CJ, but his brand is good and will no doubt pay off for him.

Learn to have spirited conversations in your mind. Take some time to process. Don't send emails, texts, or posts in the middle of your disappointment. In fact, write that heated email down, pour out everything you have to say, and send that email only to yourself. Read that email when the disappointment has paled and tension has dissipated – you know, you wouldn't have wanted to send that email now. Any and every rage-filled reaction never ends well.

- True influencers build trust by being respectful of their pain.

- They know the game is bigger than one loss.

• People will remember what you made them experience during your disappointing time.

• Learn how to handle letdowns well, and wait for the benefits.

You may feel momentarily satisfied by venting — but people remember the storm, not the relief. You can lose in five minutes what took five years to build.

Pro-tip: Your brand is revealed in moments of loss. Make sure your reactions build trust, not tension.

Handling Disappointment with Grace: Practical Tips

So, what does it look like to handle disappointment with grace? I mean most of us have almost every time reacted extremely toward hard times. For everyone wondering, here are a few practical approaches:

1. **Pause before you respond.** Give your emotions space to settle. A few hours — or even a day — can make a world of difference in how you channel your emotions.

2. **Acknowledge the loss; cut the drama.** The theatrics feel heroic in your mind, but they are ugly in reality. Be honest without being dramatic.

3. **Stay professional — even if others are not.** Kindness and professionalism are never wasted, and always rewarded in one way or another. Keep your composure even if others fall short.

4. **Look for the hidden opportunity.** Disappointments often reroute us to better paths we wouldn't have seen otherwise. What's the deeper lesson here? What is it that you hadn't noticed before?

5. **Responses reflect values.** Ask yourself: "What kind of person do I want to be remembered as in this moment?" That question alone can anchor you in composure.

Every disappointment you face is molding of your character – you can mold it beautifully or let it be a mess. So, next time you face disappointment, remember: this is your moment to deepen trust, strengthen your brand, and quietly influence those around you.

Not by what you win. But by how you carry yourself when you lose.

Pro-tip: Your professionalism in low moments becomes your reputation in high places.

Practical Takeaways

- ✓ Disappointment reveals your true character and shapes how others perceive your brand.

- ✓ People may not know the depth of your frustration, but they'll remember the way you responded.

- ✓ Handling disappointment with composure builds trust. Grace under pressure earns more influence than any loud outburst ever could.

- ✓ Impulsive reactions damage relationships and credibility. Venting may feel justified at the moment but can leave long-term scars on your brand.

- ✓ Your influence grows in quiet, thoughtful responses — not in emotional explosions. Choose poise over impulse.

- ✓ Every setback is an opportunity to strengthen your legacy. People follow those who stay grounded when things get rough.

Exercises

- ➤ Disappointment Reflection Journal: Think back to a recent moment of disappointment. Write down your answers to the following questions: What exactly disappointed me? What emotions did I feel at that moment? How did I react — verbally, emotionally, and behaviorally? Looking back, what would I do differently?

- ➢ The Brand Lens Exercise: Imagine someone else watched your reaction to your last major disappointment — maybe a colleague, client, or friend. Now answer: What would they say about your character based on how you handled it? Would they see you as composed, reactive, thoughtful, or impulsive? What story did your behavior tell about your personal brand?

- ➢ Replace the Reaction: Choose one disappointing situation from your past that you didn't handle well. Rewrite the scene: How could you have handled it with more grace? What words would you have used instead? How could you have responded in a way that maintained trust and influence?

- ➢ Emotional Response Audit: Over the next week, track your responses to small disappointments, delays, misunderstandings, and minor frustrations. Write a short log each day: What happened? How did you feel? How did you respond?

  At the end of the week, reflect: Are there patterns? What triggers impulsive behavior? What are you proud of?

Chapter 9
Proverb #8 – Be the mature one in disagreement

If we are alive and breathing, at some point, we will find ourselves in a disagreement, a conflict, a difference of opinion. There are many choices of how to handle that. I think we all know that whenever you find yourself in a conflict or disagreement, dialogue, and reasoning are always the best way out. The only intent of this chapter is to teach you how to be reasonable and mature in conflict situations.

With that being said, let's have a cursory look at our functional and dysfunctional parts of the world. I mean, of course, it's our actions, reactions, and decisions that flourish the part of the world or render it a wasteland. After decades of conflict known as 'The Troubles' in Northern Ireland, characterized by violence between Unionists and Nationalists, political leaders from both sides finally engaged in dialogue. Political leaders, including British and Irish governments, as well as Northern Ireland's political parties, engaged in extensive negotiations, listening to each other's perspectives and addressing concerns. The agreement significantly reduced violence, established devolved governance, and created a framework for lasting peace.

On the other hand, Long-standing ethnic tensions between Hutus and Tutsis escalated after the assassination of the Rwandan president. Instead of engaging in dialogue to resolve political and ethnic issues, factions resorted to violence. The conflict spiraled into genocide, resulting in the deaths of an estimated 800,000 people and leaving a lasting scar on the nation.

Fighting was, and never will be, an answer to any conflict. But still, fighting has been promoted throughout history as a means to resolve disputes, assert dominance, or protect one's beliefs. From wars between nations to personal disagreements, people often resort to confrontation rather than conversation. This pattern persists because, when our emotions are heightened or there is a perceived threat, fighting seems like the most straightforward path to victory. However, while fighting might offer a fleeting sense of power or resolution, it rarely addresses the root causes of conflict. Instead, it often leaves behind resentment, broken relationships, and unresolved issues.

In contrast, history shows that dialogue, even in the face of deep disagreement, can lead to long-lasting solutions and mutual respect. The choice between fighting and constructive dialogue ultimately shapes not only the outcome of a conflict but also the legacy it leaves behind. As individuals seeking to build trust and influence, opting for dialogue over fighting is a powerful commitment to maturity, respect, and positive change.

In a world filled with divisiveness, it's more important than ever to engage in conflict constructively. The key to breaking the cycle of 'confrontation over conversation' lies not in being louder or more forceful but in being more thoughtful.

One of the books that forever changed me was Stephen Covey's 7 Habits of Highly Successful People. Of all the great wisdom in each of the 7, I think Habit 4—Seek First to Understand, then to be Understood, was the most impactful for me. It changed how I deal with conflict, listening, and relationships. It lays out a highly effective model of being calm, putting your own needs aside for a minute, really listening, playing back for understanding, and then – and only then – sharing your perspective.

Pro-tip: Always prioritize thoughtful responses over impulsive reactions.

Listen First, Speak Second

In my experience, long before we lose logic in a conflict, we lose our sense of listening. Wherever you see conflict aplenty, know that no one listens or hears anything there. And quite frankly, listening is the most overlooked and the simplest way to resolve a conflict. Even if you disagree – your act of listening – just listening – might win you an argument that you thought was un-winnable. Most people, when faced with disagreement, immediately jump to defend their stance. So, before you sound a little out-of-control, sit back, and take in what others are saying. Take a moment to truly hear the other person's perspective, it can change the entire dynamic of the conversation. And you might be pleasantly surprised to know the others were making more sense than you.

A powerful technique is to repeat back what the other person has said, not as a means of mockery but to demonstrate that you genuinely understand their concerns. For example, saying, "If I'm hearing you correctly, you're feeling frustrated because..." shows that you respect their feelings and are trying to comprehend their point of view. This approach often diffuses tension because it acknowledges the other person's perspective without immediately countering it.

Pro-tip: Listening resolves conflicts, shows respect, and opens space for dialogue. Pause and seek to understand the other person's perspective.

Ask Clarifying Questions

Other than the charged spew of words, the thing I despise the most is 'senseless questions.' No, assumptions. Actually, both. See, one thing wastes time, and the other builds resentment. Senseless questions often come from a place of not truly listening, while assumptions arise from preconceived notions. Both are harmful because they derail conversations, lead to misunderstandings, and escalate conflicts unnecessarily. To say precisely, people with senseless questions talk when they shouldn't and people with assumptions don't talk when they should. Both shouldn't exist, in my opinion. So, the golden rule here is to ask when needed and stay quiet – so that you may not make a fool of yourself.

After showing that you've listened, it's essential to ask clarifying questions. Instead of making assumptions, seek to understand the root of the disagreement. Questions like, "Can you explain why you feel that way?" or "What would make this situation better for you?" show that you are open to finding common ground. These questions provide insight and give the other person a chance to articulate their thoughts more clearly.

Pro-tip: Ask with purpose, not just to fill the silence. Thoughtful questions lead to clarity, while assumptions create conflict.

The Concept of disagreeing with maturity '

Oh, to disagree maturely is to dance with grace, to hold your ground without losing face, to build bridges, and not stand alone, to choose respect over raw desire. To disagree well is not about winning but seeking to mend. Maturity means you both reach the end.

This concept is about prioritizing the relationship over the argument, reason over rage, dialogue over desire, and fairness over fight. It's easy to get caught up in proving your point – and your point might be the right one and deserved to be heard – still, mature conflict resolution requires a different approach. Fighting fair means taking a step back to consider the long-term impact of your words and actions. Employing this approach in no sense means surrendering to illogical arguments and wrong notions. That's the thing, this approach means bringing people who want to fight to the table and making them have a conversation. Trust me, if you do even that much, you have won.

I remember in a meeting one time, a fellow executive made a statement that our commission plan was bad, it didn't meet the needs of the company and should be abolished. You can imagine what the VP of Sales had to say about that. The next 5 minutes was a back-and-forth volley of opinions, challenges, and attempts to convince the other side of their opinion. After a while of watching this happen, I called a timeout. I asked both executives to participate in a Seek First to Understand process. They begrudgingly agreed. Here is how it went: I started by asking Exec #1 to make his statement again. I asked, "Tell me your belief about the commission plan." Before he answered, I asked Exec #2 to not say a word, but instead to listen, play back what you heard, and ask questions for clarification. But at no time could Exec #2 give her opinion on the matter. Once Exec #2 had heard all the opinions, Exec #1 felt heard. Then I allowed Exec #2 to give her opinion. In the end, it was a misunderstanding. Through calm interactions, they were able to come to an agreement, save the relationship, and be productive teammates going forward. This is not easy. It takes a lot to stay calm. We are wired to be understood after all. We want to get our points across. It is one of our greatest needs as humans. The most mature person in a disagreement has to start, stay calm, and do this right , seeking first to understand and then to be understood. Is that you? Is that part of your brand? If not, may I encourage you to start being an understander?

Pro-tip: Choose understanding over winning.
Fighting fair means valuing relationships more
than proving a point.

When Walking Away Is the Best Option

Till now, you all have at least one person in mind whom you cannot get through. That one person who has failed to listen to you. That one person who cannot resist but interrupt whenever you try to put your point across. That one person who despite being on the table confronted you over and over again. That one person you just cannot stand. Unfortunately, some of you might even have more than one person in mind. What do you do with such a person? Do you continue confronting them in hopes of convincing them? Do you try and try to prove yourself right knowing it's pointless? Do you keep arguing and exhausting yourself because you know you are right?

No, no, and absolutely no. See, even when it comes to disagree maturely, you need to know who deserves your continued energy. Mark Twain, said, "Never argue with stupid people, they will drag you down and beat you with experience." It's the same thing with hard-headed people and those who don't listen. Never argue with them, they will argue until they have exhausted you. See, such people are replete with confrontational fuel, it never depletes. In these cases, walking away is not a sign of defeat but a demonstration of self-respect and maturity. Staying in a fruitless argument only deepens resentment.

Pro-tip: The smartest response to senseless arguments is often no response at all.

Maturity Breeds Respect

Maturity, the oft overlooked and disregarded aspect, is the one gleaning respect the most. When you are composed and calculated, it often discourages the imminent confrontation. Maturity sets the tone of respect, and people reciprocate the behavior presented to them. So, the easiest way to de-escalate the confrontation is to hold your composure.

Mature disagreement is not about conceding or avoiding conflict; it's about choosing a higher path. By listening first, seeking to understand, and knowing when to walk away, you become the mature party. In the long run, this approach not only preserves relationships but also strengthens your brand as someone who values respect and integrity over momentary victory. Besides, the victory at the expense of your respect and reputation is no victory at all – it's an illusion you choose to blind yourself with. As you think about your brand, please be different...handle disagreements with calm and respect. Being different in this area will escalate your brand, and increase your influence.

Pro-tip: Stay calm, listen first, and know when to walk away — your reputation will thank you.

Practical Takeaways

- ✓ Taking the time to understand the other person's perspective can de-escalate conflict and build respect.
- ✓ Asking questions helps uncover the root of the disagreement and shows your willingness to collaborate.
- ✓ Prioritize the relationship over the argument by expressing your views without undermining the other person.

- ✓ Sometimes, removing yourself from an unproductive conflict demonstrates maturity and self-respect.
- ✓ By being the calm and respectful party, you set a positive example that can inspire others to follow.

Exercises

➢ Active Listening Practice: Think about a recent disagreement you had. Write down what the other person said and how you responded. Reflect on whether you truly listened or jumped to defend your point. How could you have responded differently?

➢ Conflict Script: Use this framework in a disagreement:

- o Step 1: "Can you explain your perspective in detail?"
- o Step 2: "Here's what I heard you say. Is that correct?"
- o Step 3: "Is there anything else I should know before I share my view?"

➢ Role Play: Imagine a scenario where someone is being confrontational. Script your responses using the principles of fighting fair — listening, clarifying, and de-escalating. Share your script with a friend and practice together.

➢ Walking Away with Grace: Describe a situation where walking away would have been the best choice. Write a short paragraph about how you would handle it now, using the maturity techniques discussed.

Chapter 10
Proverb #9 – Go Beyond the Golden Rule

"Do not impose on others what you do not wish for yourself."

Confucius.

We are all raised to believe in this Golden Rule of ethical behavior. Recall the number of times your parents – either of them – taught you or even reprimanded you saying, "That's not good; you wouldn't want someone to do that to you," or something along the lines. Trust me, I have done that too with my kids. What else are we supposed to say to teach your young ones about fairness and treating everyone fairly and nicely? We call this and believe this to be 'setting their moral compass right.' We train our kids to consider what harm or hurt their actions and words might cause others. We teach our kids to not be selfish, share with others, and always act with integrity come what may. Repeat this a thousand times over, and you will see the fruits of your efforts. You will observe your kid being polite with others, sharing with their fellows, and holding themselves back from hurting anyone. It works beautifully. So beautifully that it might well up your eyes – it really does. We all see videos on the internet about kids who act like adults at the mere age of three and can't help but praise that kid's parents for raising them so well. Those parents have prevented unnecessary harm, created civility, and fostered respect, so, "Do unto others as you would have them do unto you."

But does this rule hold for the rest of our lives?

Can we follow this through as we grow?

Is the world that fair?

Well, unfortunately, it's three no's from me. The simple explanation for this is that the world is far more complex than it was in our childhood. We need a more nuanced, more inclusive, and sometimes even exclusive aspect of this Golden Rule. See, fairness isn't always sameness. What you think is kind might be dismissive to others. What you deem as helpful might be intrusive for someone else. Golden Rule trained you to be considerate, kind, compassionate, and selfless, but the world is complicated. The Golden Rule also leaves a lot of room for assumption.

See, if you want to lead others, collaborate with them, and be the right influence, you must adopt a more nuanced standard. Rather than acknowledging your standards and preferences, you need to acknowledge **their** preferences. We need to understand what others value – and meet them there. This is where you influence others – and this is the evolved version of the Golden Rule we need now.

We know the Golden Rule is simple. It's easily memorable and it feels fair. Yet — when applied too literally — miscommunication, frustration, and conflict surface.

Think about it. If you're someone who appreciates blunt honesty, you might believe you're being respectful by giving others direct, no-nonsense feedback. "I'd want someone to tell me the truth," you think. But what if the person on the receiving end doesn't interpret bluntness as respect, but as aggression? What if their style values tact, tone, or timing?

Or consider the friend who loves big celebrations. They throw you a surprise birthday party because that's exactly what they'd want—fun, loud, and filled with people. But you feel anxious in large crowds. You smile politely, but inside you're dying to escape that party.

That is the not-so-understood paradox of the Golden Rule: rooted in good intentions, and unintentionally centering your preferences as the universal standard.

It's like giving someone your favorite Pumpkin Spiced Latte as a gift—assuming they will love it just as much as you do. They don't. You meant well, but they truly despise that flavor. Or they might even don't like coffee. It's like the Christmas sweater your grandma crocheted for you – you appreciate the effort, but you're never wearing it in front of anyone else except your grandma.

The world has evolved and it has countless diversities – you can't even begin to label someone something without knowing that surely. So, we can't go on treating people the way we like – you might like people to tell you the truth as it is, and others want the sugarcoated and digestible version of the truth. If you want to build understanding, deepen the connection, and have a meaningful relationship, then you must,

Treat people how they want to be treated.

This mindset shift is what separates good intentions from great influence. For this, empathy, adaptability, and the willingness to step outside yourself are crucial integral elements — not to change who you are, but to honor who they are.

This Golden Rule has now a not-so-known name. Lets call it the Platinum Rule. It isn't a change of semantics, it is a whole new orientation. It is like saying, "I won't assume your needs are identical to mine. I'll take the time to discover what you value."

This is about emotional maturity and intentional effort. It requires the humility to realize that your way — however thoughtful or effective it may be for you — is not automatically the best way for someone else.

Pro-tip: Sometimes, love, respect, or appreciation need to be *translated* into the recipient's emotional language.

Think of It Like Traveling with a Map

Ever been on a road trip? There is never one way or one route that all people agree to – well, even if it happens, it is a rare occasion. So, you plan a road trip – a trip that you want everyone to enjoy – but they are people with different choices and preferences. You choose a route with highways, enabling you to reach the destination quicker. However, your friends want to enjoy the entire trip, including the scenic views on the route. You and your friends are going to the same destination, but your idea of the 'best trip ever' is entirely different from them.

And we know you can't only follow your preferences. That way, you will drive past all the views your friends want to see, hence, making them feel left out and spoiling their trip. But if you follow your friends' route, you'll end up feeling frustrated and feel like 'it isn't my trip anymore.'

But what if you paused to compare maps? What if you talked about the trip? What if you aligned on goals, and compromised where necessary?

That's called adaptability – it's more like going on a trip with someone else's map. It doesn't mean you throw away your sense of direction—it means you're willing to tweak the route so that everyone feels considered, seen, and respected.

In almost every situation – be it personal or professional – adaptability makes all the difference. People want to be treated respectfully and kindly but also intentionally. They want their terms to be understood while respecting your terms. It's how humans are supposed to co-exist. In almost every, and any confrontational situation, adaptability seems like a glaring lacking.

Yet most people apply the Golden Rule assuming that it is applicable in every situation. "I like feedback right away, so I'll give it that way." "I appreciate public acknowledgment, so I'll praise my team at the next meeting." "I value alone time when I'm upset, so I'll give my friend space too." Uh, no. The Golden Rule is, was, and never will be universally satisfying. What soothes you might aggravate others. What encourages you might embarrass someone else. The clarity you seek might overwhelm the others. This is particularly necessary for influence – it isn't just kindness, it is personalized kindness, it is adaptability.

Pro-tip: You're not "losing" your way by accommodating others — you're choosing a *shared* path that builds trust.

Influence Without Imitation

Through my career, I have spent 25 years as an executive. Of the many words people have used to describe me over the years, analytical, formal, and data-driven would never be three descriptors you would ever hear. So, working with Boards of Directors has always been the most challenging part of every executive job I have ever held. Boards have a unique and extremely important role in providing oversight, strategic direction, and CEO management and succession. They are a collection of extremely successful professionals who come together regularly to accomplish their tasks in a direct, formal, timely, and efficient manner. I have made hundreds of presentations to Board over the last 25 years, and have learned a lot. Each time, I have to adjust my style to match the style of the Board. Formal, Direct, Data backing up recommendations, Timely, Efficient, and Succinct would be the words I would use to describe the "game face" I have to put on every time I present. I have enjoyed many years of working with many Boards. I have been told my "brand" with Boards has been effective through the years. I have got a lot done with Boards through the years and am proud of our accomplishments. Making that adjustment is mentally and physically tiring! That is a fact. When I am forced to adjust and adapt my style to meet the needs of others, it takes real energy. That is why many professionals schedule these kinds of high adaptation events at the start of their week or the start of their day when they are fresh and have energy to burn.

I'll repeat myself, the key to going beyond the Golden Rule is adaptability and staying authentic. You can't influence while imitating, you have to be authentic. Or you will be found out. You can't pull it off. If you are gregarious, outgoing, not detail-oriented, and don't do well with data and numbers, to try "become" a mathematician or an accountant to influence others will come off as fake. But what you can do is adapt. Just move away from your preferences a little bit to meet the needs of the person you are influencing. Be on time, limit small talk, use a slower pace, and allow them time to make a decision. All small little adaptations that will meet the needs of others, and position you for higher levels of influence with them.

Pro-tip: No one is born with adaptability. It's a trait that needs to be practiced over time.

Practical Takeaways

✓ Treating others how *you* want to be treated can sometimes miss the mark. People are different. Influence grows when you treat them how *they* want to be treated.

✓ Adjusting your style to meet others where they are isn't about losing yourself—it's about valuing connection over convenience. It shows empathy, effort, and intentionality.

✓ Whether it's how you communicate, solve problems, or show appreciation—recognize that others may have completely different preferences. Assume diversity, not sameness.

✓ You can't guess how others want to be treated. Ask. Observe. Learn. Then respond accordingly. Influence starts with listening, not assuming.

✓ Sometimes adapting feels slower or harder — but it leads to better outcomes in the long run: stronger trust, fewer misunderstandings, and deeper relationships.

✓ You're not being fake when you shift your approach. You're being wise. You're choosing to serve others in a way that honors their uniqueness, not just your defaults.

✓ The more attuned you are to others' needs and preferences, the more likely they are to trust you, follow your lead, and reciprocate that level of respect.

Exercises

➢ Style Mapping Challenge: Choose two people you interact with regularly (e.g., a colleague, friend, or family member). For each person, answer:

- How do they prefer to communicate? (e.g., text vs. phone, quick vs. detailed)
- How do they handle conflict or feedback?
- What makes them feel appreciated or understood?
- How do they express themselves emotionally?

Now, challenge yourself to adjust your next interaction with each person based on your observations.

➢ The "What Matters Most" Interview: Ask three people in your life this question: "What's one thing someone can do that makes you feel really understood and respected?" You might be surprised by the answers. Record what they say. This becomes a cheat sheet for real, personalized influence.

- ➢ Identify Your Default Lens: Everyone has a "default lens" they use to interact with the world. Take a few minutes to finish these sentences:
  - I tend to show care by _____.
  - When I'm upset, I usually _____.
  - When I want feedback, I prefer it to be _____.
  - When I communicate, I prioritize _____.

  Then ask someone close to you to fill out the same blanks. Compare notes.

- ➢ Role Reversal Scenario: Choose a relationship where communication feels strained or inconsistent. Now, do a role-reversal journaling exercise:

  Write a short paragraph from their point of view.

  - How might they perceive you?
  - What might they wish you would do differently?
  - What does "feeling respected" probably look like to them?

Chapter 11
Proverb #10 – Build Your Emotional Intelligence

The beginning of this chapter might not sit well with some people; and some people might applaud it – a little too much. But I am only sharing the following example as a 'role model', not representing any ideologies or promoting any political motive. So, during her time as First Lady, Michelle Obama encountered constant public scrutiny, political tension, and deeply personal attacks. One moment, in particular, stood out—not because of what she said, but because of how she responded. More like 'chose' to respond.

In the 2016 presidential campaign, Michelle was the target of repeated jabs and harsh rhetoric. Many expected her to fire back. Trust me, most people would have fired back, and it might be justified too, considering the personal attacks. Instead, she delivered a now-famous line in her speech at the Democratic National Convention: "When they go low, we go high."

To most, it might just seem like a slogan, knowing it was said during her campaign. However, if you were to ask me, it was a masterclass in emotional intelligence.

She could have reacted with anger, right? She could have defended herself publicly, meet negativity with further negativity, right? Uh, no. She read the emotional tone of the country. She understood that retaliation would deepen political division. She regulated her own emotions, and modeled the behavior we all must aspire. Well, some might say, her response was weak—it was actually wise - politically speaking, too - intentional, and influential.

This is emotional intelligence.

It's not about avoiding conflict or putting on a calm face. It's about understanding the emotions—yours and others'—and letting that awareness guide your words, your tone, and most importantly, your timing. People who oppose her politically, might also have applauded her that day.

See, it isn't about making headlines - conflicts might headline, big, bold, flashy headlines. But in moments that matter, it is the difference between division and understanding, between power and true influence.

Emotional Intelligence (EI) also known as Emotional Quotient (EQ) was best described in Daniel Goleman's book called Emotional Intelligence when he defined it as the ability to perceive, use, understand and handle emotions. Being able to influence others can be an emotional endeavor. You are trying to get someone to agree with your position, support your idea, give you what you think you deserve, make that sale that is so important to your family, etc. Decisions made by others are made sometimes with high emotions. Being able to perceive, understand, process and handle those emotions is an important key to influence. Being able to self-regulate, make choices about language, being sensitive to your audience, being able to "read the room" are key corollaries to the original definition. In my life, I have seen highly intelligent (IQ) individuals get stuck because they have not developed the EI abilities. Here are some examples of high EQ behaviors:

- You get your points across without offending others. You regulate your language to adapt to others. You "read the room" and choose appropriate language.
- You sense time and space. You speed up or slow down, you notice. When someone looks at their watch or their devices, you notice, and you speed up your pace accordingly.
- You make others feel comfortable, use inclusive language. Again, a choice to be sensitive to others, to predict the emotions of the person you are trying to influence.
- You are a good "team talker", involving others in discussion. You know how to not dominate, to use other people to help get points across.
- You are aware, you feel what's going on, you see things others don't.
- You allow someone else to win once in a while. Highly emotionally intelligent people don't squabble over details when it really doesn't matter. I remember vividly a colleague of mine making a presentation to a church board. He described something as happening "quickly". One of the Board members raised their hand and took issue with their description and thought the word "swiftly" would

better describe the point they were making. Are you kidding me right now? I remember my colleague feeling deflated, confused and just generally annoyed by that comment. That is a perfect example of low EQ. To feel like you just need to win so bad that you have to just change a word to hear yourself talk...was a demonstration of what we are talking about here. If we choose to win and not apply EQ, our influence will be lower...it just will.

Emotional Intelligence matters more than you might think, and mastering it can change not just how others see you – but how you see yourself.

Pro-tip: True influence isn't about reacting louder – it's about responding smarter.

The Power of Perception

Like most things in life, EQ also begins with awareness. This means noticing not only what is being said but how it's being said. In reality, 'how' is the crucial part of every conversation, meeting or interview you ever had. Ever noticed?

High EQ individuals pick up on expressions, body language, tone, and pacing. They notice the hesitations, the sighs, the subtle cues, the roll of the eye, and the hidden emotion behind 'can I have some water?'. This perceptiveness helps them read emotional undercurrents in any situation.

For example, someone might say "I'm fine," but their shoulders are tense, their voice is flat, and they avoid eye contact. Or they said that in a rather pitched tone. A person with strong emotional perception won't take that 'fine' as is, they will pick up on the emotional mismatch. Maybe that person is frustrated, hurt, or overwhelmed, but not ready to say so. High EQ individuals notice that something is off, and they tweak their responses accordingly.

You can also observe emotions as a group energy. In meetings or team discussions, High EQ individuals sense when people are disengaged, when tension is building, or when someone wants to speak but doesn't feel safe to. They pay attention to the unsaid, and allow space for those emotions to emerge.

This level of perceptiveness is like having a sixth sense. It doesn't come from being nosy or overly analytical — it comes from being present. When you are truly in that moment, not just for yourself but for others, too. You can't read emotional cues if you're distracted, rushing, or fixated on your own thoughts. High EQ individuals are observers, in the best way: calm, curious, and tuned in.

Throughout my career I have been a part of many acquisitions. Acquisitions are a blend of data, financing, the "art of the deal," and very cerebral stuff. Noone would ever describe my role in acquisitions to be on the cerebral side! However, I remember many times meetings owners who had built very successful companies. They were a group to be honored and respected. I remember one of my first acquisitions I was ever assigned to. I was the HR guy on the due diligence team meeting with the owner for the first time. We dove into the deal – the data, the financing, the transition, the earnout, the expectations, the purchase agreement, the regulations. About an hour into that meeting, I knew something was off. The owner was not enthusiastic, non-cooperative, non-responsive, and overall just not in a good place. I called a time out and asked the owner a question, "Mr. Owner, as you think about this possible acquisition, what is keeping you up at night?" That question hit him like a cool drink of water on a hot day. He took a deep breath and said, "My people. I want to make sure my people are cared for, treated well, respected, and they have pathways for their growth." He was also concerned about losing the culture they had built and their position in the communities they served. I think I have been blessed with some pretty good EQ. As I asked him questions, played back his responses, then shared with him our assurances for his people. After that conversation, he was ready to talk about the deal.

Always read the room. Perceive the emotions. Listen with your eyes, not your ears. Have the courage to dive into areas that may be off the agenda, that is EQ.

Pro-tip: Sometimes, the most emotionally intelligent thing you can do is wait. A slight pause gives you space to respond with more care and clarity.

Understanding Emotions – Yours & Theirs

Perception is powerful, but it is just the flimsy first layer. True emotional intelligence lies in interpretation. It's one thing to notice someone's crossed arms or hesitation—it's another to identify why they feel that way and what they might need.

Emotionally intelligent people know that emotions are rarely simple or one-dimensional. Frustration, for instance, might be a cover for fear. Anger might shell a sense of shame. Confidence might be masking insecurity. Yeah, seems paradoxical, but it is true. People with high EQ don't jump to conclusions—they look deeper, asking themselves, "What else could be going on here?"

They also apply this same awareness for themselves. You aren't supposed to be good at reading others—you should first know how to read yourself. They know their triggers, recognize when they project their stress onto others, and take responsibility for their internal state.

This awareness builds a foundation for empathy, clarity, and better decision-making. It alters your system to respond instead of react. To clarify instead of assume. To create safety instead of tension.

To say it simply, it is all about sensitivity and courage. Having the sensitivity to identify clues in others regarding 'where they are at?' and then having the courage to step into uncomfortable spots to listen and understand really what is going on. Low EQ people lack sensitivity. They just plow forward and have a mantra of 'this is how I am' and that's why they hold no true influence. True influence comes when someone believes that you have perceived their emotions and handled them well.

If you want to know yourself better, take an EQ assessment. Try on your own to intentionally listen with your eyes, look for non verbals and self-regulate accordingly. Honestly, many of us will not be able to do this alone. Improving your own EQ is challenging. Find a mentor that has high EQ. Ask them to help you perceive and regulate. Have them attend an event with you, have them attend a meeting, ask them for feedback on the clues you missed and tips to do better.

And trust me on this, those who commit to it, EQ becomes not just a tool for success, but a way of living with greater integrity and humanity…and ultimately influence.

Pro-tip: Whether it is frustration or fear, labeling emotions – yours or others' – creates clarity.

Practical Takeaways

- ✓ Emotional intelligence isn't about suppressing emotions—it's about understanding and using them wisely to build trust, connection, and impact.
- ✓ High EQ begins with noticing—tone, timing, body language, and what's *not* being said. It's about seeing beyond the surface.
- ✓ The emotionally intelligent pause. They choose their words and tone with intention, especially in high-stakes or emotionally charged situations.
- ✓ Leading with empathy—like Michelle Obama did—isn't weakness. It's a strategic, human-centered approach that inspires deeper respect and influence.
- ✓ Small choices—like letting someone else win, adjusting your pace, or choosing inclusive language—signal emotional maturity and build credibility.
- ✓ Unlike IQ, EQ can be developed. Through awareness, practice, and feedback, emotional intelligence becomes not just a skill—but a mindset.

Exercises

- ➢ Mirror Moments (Daily Emotional Check-In): Each morning or evening, pause for 2 minutes in front of a mirror and ask yourself:
  - • What emotion am I feeling right now?
  - • What triggered it?
  - • How is this emotion influencing my behavior or decision-making today?

➢ Empathy Walk: Choose someone you interact with regularly (a colleague, employee, or family member). Spend one day consciously trying to see the world through their lens. Ask:
- What might they be worried about today?
- What pressures or feelings might they be carrying?

➢ The "Pause and Pivot" Challenge: For one week, anytime you feel triggered—annoyed, offended, impatient—pause for 5 seconds before responding. Ask:
- Am I about to react or respond?
- What would an emotionally intelligent version of me do right now?

➢ EQ Journaling (End-of-Day Review): At the end of each day, write a short reflection:
- What was one emotionally charged moment I handled well today?
- What would I do differently next time?
- What EQ skill did I use (awareness, regulation, empathy, adaptability)?

Chapter 12
Proverb #11 – Develop a "Yes, If" Mentality

Before I jump into how mentality and mindset affect leadership, I need you to really think about the kind of mindset you have.

When you speak, do people lean in, roll their eyes, or shut down?

When a challenge arises, do you look for solutions or get stuck on the problems?

When someone proposes an idea, are you the person who encourages it or dismisses it?

It represents whether you can be trusted with progress.

Can you move things forward when plans change?

Can you hold space for ideas that aren't your own?

Can you respond to pressure with calm, and to conflict with clarity?

These subtle signals speak louder than any heavily referenced resume, articulated speech, or even your intention. It shows whether you're an accelerator or a barrier, whether you want to build bridges or build higher walls. Over time, those signals either open doors or quietly close them.

We may not realize it, but our every action constantly broadcasts a message about our mindset. It is how the people around us experience us, and sets if they want to continue with that experience. It reflects whether you are someone who creates momentum or someone who resists everything positive happening around you. And you don't realize this, but over time, this mental posture becomes your identity, your brand.

As much as we deem 'titles' significant, people don't stick to 'people with titles'; they follow people with vision, belief, and clarity.

This is why mindset is often considered the quiet engine behind great leadership. It doesn't scream. It is about how you respond to pressure, how you treat others, how you approach the uncertainties, and your decisions, especially when it's inconvenient. Leaders who consistently generate trust and influence are rarely the smartest in the room, but they almost always have the strongest mindset.

They've trained themselves to stay open.

To look for solutions.

To lead with curiosity instead of control.

To adapt quickly.

To react smartly.

To keep their composure intact, regardless of the circumstances.

As much as we want to believe this, leadership isn't a position. Yes, read that again. Leadership doesn't equate to executive or managerial positions. Leadership begins with a mindset. Yes, read it again, emphasis on mindset. Leadership is a way of seeing the world with clarity, responding to it with purpose, and creating possibilities.

Your mindset is the invisible force shaping your behavior, your tone, your decisions, and ultimately your brand. It also influences whether people experience you as a problem-solver or a problem-creator, a door-opener or a gatekeeper.

In every conversation, every project, every challenge, people expect a certain kind of thinking from you. And over time, that thinking becomes your leadership fingerprint. Not your résumé. Not your skills. Your mindset.

And here is the tough fact to accept. People who move the world forward, who create possibilities, who deal with challenges smartly, who earn trust, and who inspire change—don't always have all the answers. So, if they don't have the answers, what makes them the leader, you wonder. Their approach and their right attitude. That "Yes, if" mentality makes all the difference.

Most of us are surrounded by "No, because" thinkers. You hear them say:

"No, because we tried that last year."

"No, because the budget won't allow it."

"No, because the timing's off."

"No, because we've tighter deadlines."

"No, because we don't have enough resources."

And I am not saying these reasons are baseless or untrue — they might be totally valid. But they shut the conversation down. They are focused on what can't be done.

The "Yes, if" mentality changes the script entirely. It says:

"Yes, we can try that, if we adjust the scope."

"Yes, that could work, if we add more resources."

"Yes, let's do it, if we secure leadership buy-in."

See the difference? See how such simple statements open up possibilities. It turns dead ends into bridges.

Pro-tip: Speak in terms of possibilities and adjustments, not just limitations.

Reframing is Influence

It's appalling how people still assume influence is all about authority or control. If you have influence, that means you have a certain kind of control over people - to mold their mindsets, to shape their ideas, and to make or break their lives. The word 'influence' itself is said with a rather negative connotation. I believe influence was never said with an implication of 'helping others', 'helping people see a future they didn't see before.'

I bet you never heard that implication of 'influence.' Right?

Here's the truth: Real influence is earned, not imposed - authority is imposed, not influence. And those are two different things.

Rerouting, when you reframe a conversation from "No, because…" to "Yes, if…", you're applying strategic leadership. You acknowledge the constraints while refusing to be controlled by them. That is what makes this 'Yes, if' mindset so powerful.

It is not blind optimism. It's a 'possibility with a plan.'

It's like you're saying:

"I acknowledge the obstacles. I'm not ignoring them. But I believe there's a path—and here's what I believe it would take to overcome this obstacle."

Even such statements have a profound effect on whoever you're talking to. It shows a calm authority, a will to adapt, an intent to adapt, and most importantly, being there with others.

That kind of thinking makes people feel safe, seen, and supported. And that ultimately builds trust.

Pro-tip: Let your influence be reflected from presence and posture, not position or title

---

Why "Yes, If" Builds Stronger Teams

When it comes to teams, we all need people who can think bigger, better ideas, come up with effective solutions, and have a progress mindset. Trust me, people with a 'No, because' mindset can't progress, and don't let others progress.

It doesn't always necessarily sound rude, but a 'No, because' mindset doesn't let ideas breathe or nurture.

It drains momentum.

It turns energy into frustration.

It stifles creativity.

And it erodes trust.

People naturally stop contributing their opinions or ideas as they always anticipate rejection. Even if it is a brainstorming session, people almost always end the session with the same problem with what they started the session. Meetings become less about solutions and more about surviving the hour. Eventually, progress slows to a mere crawl — if even that is possible. And this regression is not because the team lacks skills or teamwork, but because the environment lacks psychological safety, and the culture doesn't allow the ideas to grow.

In stark contrast, a "Yes, if" changes everything.

It shows that challenges are real, but not final.

It encourages people to think beyond roadblocks.

It allows people to nurture new ideas.

Most importantly, it 'listens', 'sees', and appreciates.'

A "Yes, if' mindset is how you build a culture of possibility, not one of permission.

- Pro-tip: Set a cultural tone where curiosity is encouraged and progress is expected.

How This Mindset Sparked My Business Journey

I really do expect – and hope – that up till now at least one of the proverbs in this book has altered your life, encouraged you, or maybe just made you a little happy (at least). I chose this particular proverb because it touched my life when I started contemplating starting my own business in 2002. Yeah, yeah, you might think 'here's another soppy or brag story,' – be it, here is the story.

I had a friend of mine who walked the path with me to decide whether and how to launch this life-changing endeavor. I was excited, but mainly scared and nervous – for obvious reasons. How could I possibly do this and put my family at risk to the level that I needed to make this work? He introduced me to the idea of brainstorming using a "Yes, if" mentality. Every idea, every concern, every concept had to be answered with a "Yes, if" mentality. For example:

Can we get financing? Yes, if we find the right partner.

Will customers recognize us as a valid business? Yes, if we implement good marketing and sales.

Can I really make it financially? Yes, if I establish a budget that works within proper frameworks.

You see how that works? Even just answering these difficult questions differently, you start focusing on solutions, possibilities, and an encouragement to do better. I just answered these conundrums a bit differently, and it made a huge difference.

So, the next time you get on with an endeavor, just answer your problems with "Yes, if" statements.

Pro-tip: Pair every "No, if" with a "Yes, if" to reorient your thinking toward solutions.

The Natural Law in Action

The natural law here is simple: Your mindset shapes your influence. People are always – always - drawn to people who bring possibilities to the table and stay miles away from people who offer roadblocks or highlight dead ends. By choosing "Yes, if," you position yourself as a problem-solver, not a problem-pointer.

That's how trust is built.

That's how brands are formed.

And that's how real influence grows.

Pro-tip: Show up with possibilities, not problems

Practical Takeaways

- ✓ The way you respond to challenges influences how others see you. "Yes, if" thinkers are viewed as solution-oriented, empowering, and trustworthy.
- ✓ While "No, because" stops momentum, "Yes, if" keeps conversations moving and opens the door to innovation — even in the face of real obstacles.
- ✓ Saying "Yes, if" doesn't ignore problems — it acknowledges them while guiding others toward solutions. This builds credibility and positions you as a constructive leader.
- ✓ In group settings, the "Yes, if" mindset encourages collaboration, creative thinking, and shared ownership of results.
- ✓ People remember how you frame problems. Becoming a "Yes, if" person helps shift your brand from resistant to resourceful.
- ✓ You can train yourself to reframe. Whether in work, relationships, or personal challenges, look for ways to say "Yes, if" and watch your influence grow.

Exercises

- ➢ Reframe 5 Negatives

- • Write down five common "No, because" thoughts or statements you've used recently (e.g., "No, because I don't have time").

- Reframe each one into a "Yes, if" version (e.g., "Yes, I can do that if I schedule it for next week.").

- Reflect: How does your attitude shift when you reframe the issue?

➢ The "Yes, If" Journal – 7-Day Challenge

- For one week, track daily situations where you instinctively said (or wanted to say) "no."

- Each time, write the "Yes, if" version in a journal.

- At the end of the week, review your entries:

  o Which reframes led to action or deeper conversation?

  o Did any open up surprising opportunities?

➢ Group Exercise: Idea Expansion

- In a group (team meeting, family dinner, classroom), pose a bold or unrealistic idea.

- Go around the group, and have each person respond with "Yes, if…" statements.

- Watch how ideas evolve as conditions and possibilities are added.

- Debrief: How did the mood and energy of the conversation change?

➢ Influence Roleplay

- Think of a recurring conversation where you tend to respond with skepticism (e.g., during a team brainstorm, or when your child suggests something ambitious).

- Roleplay both responses:

  o First, answer with "No, because…"

  o Then, re-answer using "Yes, if…"

- Reflect: Which version positions you as a person of influence? Which one encourages trust and solutions?

➢ Build a "Yes, If" Habit Trigger

- Choose a daily trigger that reminds you to practice the mindset (e.g., every time you check your email or hear a complaint).

- Each time the trigger happens, stop and mentally turn a "no" into a "yes, if."

- Keep a log or habit tracker for reinforcement

Chapter 13
Proverb #12 – Be A 'One-Ask' Person

"Dependability is the heartbeat of trust."

If I were to ask you, 'How do you want people to see you?' I know, I will get a thousand responses ranging from kind, loving, like a friend, some would even say, 'baddie', 'sassy', going all the way to 'unhinged', 'feral', and 'hot mess.' Seriously, the world has 'invented' more words, especially 'adjectives', than in the entire history of humanity – metaphorically speaking. So, yes, people would come up with all kinds of things to define and 'flaunt' themselves as. But if I were to suggest how one should want people to see themselves, it would be 'trustworthy' and 'dependable'.

There are only a few things that are more precious than having a trustworthy person around you. Too much? Let me put this in everyday terms. Think about that one person in your life who always shows up on time, with what they promised, no drama, no reminders, and definitely no excuses. You breathe easier when they're involved. You start depending on them to make your everyday stress a little bearable. Whether it's a group project, a family emergency, or a flat tire at midnight, they're the first person you think to call – and almost never disappoint. Why? Because they're dependable. And in a world obsessed with image, flair, and performance, that kind of quiet reliability is rare, powerful, and should be cherished as is. Imagine not having at least one such person in your life.

Now flip the lens: What if *you* were that person for others? Not just someone who's fun at parties or interesting on social media, but someone whose name evokes calm, confidence, and competence. That is what being trustworthy and dependable gives you — it builds a personal brand that speaks louder than any aesthetic, quirk, or caption ever could.

Because while being 'sassy,' 'unhinged,' or 'a hot mess' might get laughs or likes, being dependable gets you something far more valuable: influence, opportunity, and lasting respect.

When it comes to relationships, be it professional or personal, trust is that invisible glue that keeps teams united and relationships intact. It's what allows people to collaborate, take risks, and move forward together. But we all know we don't instinctively start trusting people. And trust doesn't materialize out of thin air — it's built slowly, brick by brick, day by day through consistent behavior. And at the core of that behavior is dependability.

Yes, trust and dependability are intertwined, but are two entirely different things. Just like a heartbeat keeps a body alive and functioning, dependability keeps trust alive. Without a steady beat, the system breaks down. Without dependability, trust flatlines.

Dependability doesn't have to be flashy. Well, it is never flashy. It doesn't call attention to itself. But it speaks volumes in silence. It means:

- You do what you say you'll do.

- You show up when it matters.

- You follow through, even when no one is watching.

Dependability turns promises into proof. It converts intention into action. And it makes people feel safe – people relying on you, not once, but repeatedly, and eventually, habitually.

Consider a team working on a deadline. One person drops the ball—suddenly, the whole project wobbles. Momentum slows. Doubts creep in. People stop focusing on the work and start focusing on managing each other's inconsistencies.

Now imagine that same team, but every person is dependable. No chasing. No micromanaging. The environment breathes. Progress flows. Everyone's dream team, right?

See, the more dependable someone is, the less others have to worry, wonder, or wait. That's the essence of trust. That's what I would suggest you strive to be. You can learn and earn however much you want in this world, but nothing stands nearly as valuable as someone's trust in you – and of course, your dependability is equally precious to others.

Pro-tip: True dependability shows when the going gets tough. Be the person who doesn't disappear when it gets real.

What Is a "One Ask" Person?

You have the idea what dependability entails, but dependability, when anticipated, reminded, and needs constant nagging, becomes a nuisance. Allow me to say this in simpler terms. When you know you can depend on someone, say for a project deadline, but that person needs to be reminded about the deadline. You need to keep asking them, 'When can I expect this to be delivered?' and they keep replying with 'Soon enough. Give me another hour.' And that hour passes, and another hour passes before you receive the project.

That means you are dependable but not what I have come to call a 'One Ask' person. A 'One Ask' person is someone who, when given a task or responsibility, follows through accurately, efficiently, and without needing to be reminded.

This might seem to suggest perfection, but it is really about consistency. It is about showing that when you say "I've got it," and you mean it.

Pro-tip: Beat others to the follow-up. If someone
has to ask twice, you've already lost points.

The Power of First Impressions — and Follow-Through

I'll get to this with an example. Think of two employees:

• Alex, who always delivers on time, with no need for nudging.

• Jamie, who's brilliant but often misses deadlines or needs reminders.

Who would you trust with a big client? Who would you recommend for a promotion? And who would you ask for help? It's obvious, isn't it?

Being a 'One Ask' person sends a strong message: you respect others' time. No one likes to repeat themselves, save them their words. This trait stands out in a world where so many over-promise and under-deliver.

I was asked to look back over my career and number the people who have gone on to senior-level positions and why. As I looked back over my career and thought about the hundreds of employees who have worked with me, I came to realize the ones who consistently rose to the top, had influence, and got promoted were the ones who held one attribute in common — they were a

'One Ask' person. I never had to ask them twice to do a task, lead an initiative, come up with a plan, etc.

Pro-tip: 'One Ask' people don't self-promote;
their consistency does the work.

Reliability Builds Influence

I guess, till this point, it's well-established that leadership isn't about getting the highest title; it is about earning trust. In case you were only chasing the title, you got leadership all wrong. You can get all the titles you want, but you would never be considered or looked up to as a leader. It's the people's trust in you that makes you a leader. When people know you'll show up and follow through, your influence grows naturally.

Imagine you are part of a team project. If you are the one who always takes notes, sends summaries, and completes your portion on time, your teammates will start relying on you. Over time, they'll seek your input more. You won't need to push your way into influence — you'll earn it.

Also, if you notice, when you have such a team of 'One Ask' people, the whole team starts mirroring the energy of their members. A single "One Ask" person can change the dynamic.

Now, imagine the impact of the 'One Ask' team. When others see you handle responsibilities without complaint, delay, or excuse, it subtly creates a pressure to rise to the same standard.

This is leadership by example — without fanfare or titles.

Pro-tip: When you consistently deliver, others will feel inspired — or quietly pressured — to elevate their game.

Your Brand Is Built One Ask at a Time

Your brand is not your resume. It's not your Instagram bio. It's what people say to you about you. It's what people say when you are not in the room.

Do people appreciate your commitment to deadlines?

Or do people criticize your unnecessary delays?

Do people wish for you to be on their team?

Or do people hope you aren't on their team?

Being a "One Ask" person is one of the quickest ways to build a brand of trust and excellence.

Remember, people talk about those who follow through. Know that opportunities come to those who deliver. And trust is earned – 'one ask' at a time.

Pro-tip: Ask yourself: "Would I recommend me?"

In a noisy world, dependability is rare—and therefore, powerful. Being a "One Ask" person isn't about being everyone's favorite or being perfect. Far from it; it is about showing up consistently, standing tall, and delivering when it matters.

Whether you're climbing the career ladder, running a business, or trying to strengthen relationships, this single shift— this small promise to be dependable—can change everything. In my experience, "One Ask" people outpace their peers, and gain the influence they seek. Consider striving to be described as a "One Ask" person!

"Don't strive to be impressive. Strive to be consistent. The rest will follow."

Practical Takeaways

✓ Don't rely on memory; use a system.

✓ Handle small tasks within 24 hours.

✓ If delays happen, speak up before being reminded.

✓ Replace vague responses with clear timelines.

✓ Reflect daily on your follow-through and reliability.

✓ Only commit to what you can truly deliver.

✓ Use a simple tracker to monitor tasks and build habits.

✓ Publicly show and acknowledge "One Ask" actions.

✓ Reinforce the culture by recognizing it.

✓ Reflect on whether others trust your follow-through.

Exercises

➢ The "Ask Audit" (Awareness Building): Over the next 3 days, write down every request or commitment made to you.

- Track:

    o Who asked?

    o What was the request?

    o Did you complete it on time?

    o Were you reminded?

- At the end of Day 3, ask yourself:

    o How many tasks did I deliver without reminders?

- Where did I fall short?

- What's one behavior I can improve?

➢ The "One Ask" Challenge (Behavior Training): Build the habit of follow-through.

- For 7 days, commit to this rule: no one should have to remind you twice.

- Log every task or request and mark when you complete it.

- If you anticipate a delay, proactively notify the requester.

- At the end of the challenge, reflect:

  - What felt different?

  - How did others respond to me?

  - What did I learn about my time management?

➢ Accountability Mirror: Reflect honestly on how others perceive your reliability.

- Ask 2–3 trusted coworkers, friends, or mentors:

  - "When I commit to something, do you feel confident I'll follow through?"

  - "Do you ever feel you need to follow up with me?"

- Write down their feedback without defensiveness.

- Identify one change you can make based on their responses.

➢ Language Shift Practice: Train yourself to speak with more commitment.

- For one week, replace weak phrases like "I'll try" or "Hopefully I can" with strong, clear ones like:

  o "I'll have that done by Friday."

  o "You can count on me for this."

- At the end of the week, note:

  o How it changed your mindset

  o How others responded

➢ Create Your "One Ask" Tracker: Build consistency through systems.

- Create a simple table with:

  o Task | Requester | Due Date | Status | Notes

- Use it daily to track tasks, ensure follow-through, and note when you proactively communicated delays.

- Review weekly to spot patterns and progress.

Chapter 14
Redefining My Brand

Have I perfected my life by applying all these proverbs?

Am I the absolute manifestation of all or any of these proverbs?

Have I re-evaluated, re-oriented, and reset my life according to these proverbs?

And do I now have the right to lecture anyone not living according to these proverbs?

Uh, no – all four no's. See, life isn't lived in black and white, it's mostly lived in the greys and all the colors in between. All these proverbs are there to find the best 'grey' and 'color' to live your life with. I hope this makes sense. There'll be days when I will find myself slipping away, doing things I thought I wouldn't do. But do I repeat those mistakes, or do I stay stuck with those misdemeanors?

So, I have a confession to make. This book isn't the 'bible' that will fix every wrong in your life, and heal every rift in your relationships. This is for your help, a guide to help you take those crucial first steps, the ones that lead you toward more influence, stronger trust, and a clearer sense of who you really are. Trust me, it's not magic—it's all about 'movement.' And sometimes, that movement starts with something as simple (and as hard) as asking better questions, listening a little more, or showing up, especially when it's tough.

In the first chapter of this book, I asked you to consider your brand, your reputation, the honest opinion that others have of you, and your influence. I hope you took me up on the challenge to ask people you trust to give you an honest assessment of your brand and whether it is holding you back or accelerating you forward. In the chapters of this book, I gave you 12 attributes that I have seen consistently exist in the people who have high influence.

Now, if you're anything like me, some of those attributes probably hit a little too close to home—maybe exposed a few blind spots or made you pause and think, "Yikes, do I actually do that?" That's a good thing. This isn't about being perfect; it's about being aware. Influence isn't built in a day—it's built in the choices you make every day, the way you treat people, and the habits you reinforce (or finally let go of). So, if you've stumbled along the way, welcome to the club. You're still in the right place.

Before we close our conversation, here is my challenge for you. Are you:

- Willing to redefine your brand and try some or all of the Proverbs we have discussed?
- Showing up "Memorable" every day?
- Choosing an "I am Second" mentality once in a while?
- Learning the art of "Wow"?

- Saying "Yes" every chance you get?
- Adopting a mindset that you are NEVER wasting time?
- Developing a "Giver" mindset?
- Never burning bridges?
- Being the mature party in disagreements?
- Going beyond the Golden Rule?
- Building your emotional intelligence?
- Developing a "Yes, If" mindset?
- Being a "One Ask" person?

I want to thank you for reading this book and being open to the ideas presented. True influence comes naturally to those whose brand is typified by some or all of the Proverbs we have discussed. I wish you all the best in your personal and professional journeys. Be memorable, develop your brand, and enjoy the influence it brings.

www.ingramcontent.com/pod-product-compliance
Lightning Source LLC
Chambersburg PA
CBHW051314120626
46547CB00015B/2229